CHERYL OREGLIA

GROW DAMN IT!
THE FEEDING AND NURTURING OF LIFE

Black Rose Writing | Texas

©2023 by Cheryl Oreglia
All rights reserved. No part of this book may be reproduced, stored in a retrieval system or transmitted in any form or by any means without the prior written permission of the publishers, except by a reviewer who may quote brief passages in a review to be printed in a newspaper, magazine or journal.

The author grants the final approval for this literary material.

First printing

The views and opinions expressed in this book are those of the authors and do not necessarily reflect the official policy or position of the publisher or any parties mentioned hereafter. While every effort is made to ensure that the content of this book is accurate, the information is provided "as is" and the author and publisher make no representations or warranties in relation to the accuracy or completeness of the information found within

ISBN: 978-1-68513-144-9
PUBLISHED BY BLACK ROSE WRITING
www.blackrosewriting.com

Printed in the United States of America
Suggested Retail Price (SRP) $20.95

Grow Damn It! is printed in Garamond Premier Pro

*As a planet-friendly publisher, Black Rose Writing does its best to eliminate unnecessary waste to reduce paper usage and energy costs, while never compromising the reading experience. As a result, the final word count vs. page count may not meet common expectations.

For Ann and Dick Johnson

Praise for

GROW DAMN IT!

"Generative, charming, irreverent… *Grow Damn It!* bristles with humor, emerging from the grit of real life, a spirited, yet fertile debut novel by Cheryl Oreglia."
–Nancy Slonim Aronie, author of *Memoir as Medicine,* founder of Chilmark Writing Workshop on Martha's Vineyard

"I love Cheryl Oreglia's writing. I am a long-time reader of her blog and thoroughly enjoy her stories, insights, wisdom, and humor. Cheryl is smart and sassy, and her stories make me smile. Her stories also make me think, feel, and pause a moment to reflect on issues—big and small—that truly matter. Life is busy, complicated, and can be very stressful. Cheryl's writing reminds us to experience all of it with an open mind and an open heart."
–Maryanne Pope, author of *A Widow's Awakening*
Founder & CEO of Pink Gazelle Productions Inc and the Co-Founder of the John Petropoulos Memorial Fund

"This gem of a book is a savvy guide to living a life of intention. Chock-full of inspiration, *Grow Damn It!*, will help you become the person you want to be. Keep it close by because Oreglia—a caring, inspiring, and knowledgeable companion—is a welcome and joyful presence as you journey toward self-discovery and transformation."
–Laurie Buchanan, Ph.D., author of
Note to Self: A Seven-Step Path to Gratitude and Growth

"Vignettes and slices of life that will touch your heart, make you laugh, and sometimes cry—but, mostly, laugh. From tales of life, loss, values, victories, kids, road trips, and wine—always wine, Oreglia's mini memoirs are guaranteed to captivate and entertain. I highly recommend this read! Sit down and savor these stories and *Grow Damn It!*, while living vicariously through Cheryl's journeys of life. I love her attitude and wit and am already looking forward to her next book!"

–D.G. Kaye, author of
Twenty Years: After 'I Do'–Reflections on Love and Changes Through Aging

"*Grow Damn It!* is a collection of essays by Cheryl Oreglia, she has a gift for calling out the most ridiculous and joyous aspects of life. Her relatable stories will appeal to any cynic with a sense of humor. She's beloved by many for outrageous, gut-busting rants about people and situations struggling with the mundane and the extraordinary. Cheryl takes familiar experiences and spins them into comedy gold."

–Tasha Oldham, an Emmy nominated, Directors Guild of America Award-winning filmmaker, creator of *My Story, Inc.*

"I challenge you to read through Cheryl's honest writing about life and not chuckle to yourself now and then. She's not poking fun of anyone but herself, but we can all relate. This book is full of short slice-of-life pieces that are engaging and entertaining while offering little nuggets of wisdom along the way. They're best read in spaces, like pops of candy between meals. In these tasty morsels you'll find the courage you need to keep going down your own rutted path."

–Colleen M. Story, author of *The Beached Ones*

*"And gradually you'll bloom
For - it takes time for a flower
To bloom"*
—Mairaj Fatima

CONTENTS

Introduction

PART I: Foundational
Living In the Gap
She Told Me I Could Fly
Happy Birthday Daddy
After You Say I Do
This is a Woman to Love
The Family Tree
My Daughter Shows Up at the House With Two Dead Fish
Clearlake
He Had Me At "A Substantial Rounded Becoming"

PART II: Transitional
True Grit
25 Things I Wish I Had Asked My Parents
Midlife, Nettles, and Rocking Chairs
Ten Misconceptions About Middle-Aged
The Meaning of Life
Middle-Aged Penance
It's A Jungle Out There
Grow Damn It!

PART III Monumental
When You Hit Rock Bottom
The Arrogance of Time
The Merry-Go-Round
Life Turns on Small Choices
David Calvin Wood
I'll See You Down The Road
Life Is Terminal

PART IV: Provisional
Can I Tell You About My Day
Give It A Rest
Not That You Asked
The Letters
Honey, I'm Home Forever
Tough Times Don't Last Tough People Do
I'm Sitting In Her Place

PART V: Recreational
The Larry Factor
Colons Before Coffee
Must Love Dogs
Spoiler Alert
Standing in the Parking Lot of Life
Trust Your Husband
Built To Last
She's Not Pedaling
What Do I Really Want

Epilogue

GROW DAMN IT!

INTRODUCTION

*"Gap... A gesture, incomplete! Something unfinished,
Left. A trust of heart, Faith!"*
–Tahreem Rahat

Speaking of gaps...

It is a murderously hot summer day.

We're hustling to get the entire house cleared out before having our hardwood floors refurbished for the first time in twenty years. Go easy. Housekeeping is not my thing.

It's the day after my retirement luncheon at Notre Dame, the day after a mass shooting at the VTA, and the day before, we're meeting up with Mary, Jim, Jill, and Steve at Phyllis and Greg's beach house in Capitola.

I'm sure they told us, but I missed the memo or simply forgot. The floors are now being refurbished tomorrow, which means we need to move all the furniture out of the entire house today. Of course, my husband's back goes out (how convenient), our dog refuses to stay out from underfoot, and now I have unexplainable bruises all over my body, yet my son Dante did all the heavy lifting.

I feel uneasy driving away from the empty house, with most of our belongings stacked forlornly in the backyard and Dante acting as guardian.

What could go wrong?

After spending the entire weekend in Capitola trying to recapture our youth, drinking too much wine, eating rich food, and staying up way past our bedtime. We may have overstayed our welcome at Zelda's. It happens. I believe it's going to take a week to recover and maybe some therapy.

Sunday afternoon, we head home to check on the house and collect the dog so we can spend the rest of the week up at the lake while they continue to sand and polyurethane the floors. After being stuck in beach traffic for hours, we arrive at our house feeling agitated, and as if a crime scene, a profusion of yellow tape is blocking all the doors.

I'll admit it is unsettling.

To set the crime scene a little better, the only two rooms not being refurbished are the master suite and guest room (which Dante is occupying), at opposite ends of the house. Not that it's a big house, but it has two ends.

We need to resupply our wardrobes before heading to the lake, but the master room is locked, and we cannot get there from the guest room without trapping across the freshly polyurethaned floors.

With one exception... there is a small window in the back of the house, which was left open.

Are you thinking what I'm thinking?

The next thing I know, Larry and Dante are lifting me eight feet into the air as they attempt to shove me through a one-foot by one-foot opening. I want you to appreciate, maybe even savor, the image of a sixty-year-old woman being forced to wiggle through an unimaginably small portal.

If the image is making you nauseous, you have it right.

I squeeze my arms, head, and upper torso through the tiny opening as if attempting to shove a fat finger through a small ring, and I get stuck at the knuckle halfway through the gap.

I panic, imagining the quartet of handsome firefighters who will confront my generous ass, dangling precariously from the side of the house. Remember the guy who got stuck in the Nutty Putty cave in Utah? Same thing, but I'm absolutely positive I'll never get out.

Larry and Dante are laughing as if schoolboys as they haphazardly attempt to push me through the tight opening.

Incredibly rude given my age and complete lack of dignity.

I shift my hips perpendicular to the narrow space and somehow manage to slip through, landing roughly headfirst onto the bed. It was not pretty, elegant, or applaudable.

This is exactly how I feel about life. From beginning to end, we're forced to slip through impossibly tight portals. If you've ever given birth, you'll identify with this excruciating imagery.

The thing is, we're all dangling from the edifices of life. It's not pretty, but with a generous shift, we manage to wiggle through. However, few of us nail the landing.

Grow Damn It! is about egressing our own traumatic, life-threatening, and challenging events, but emerging with an enlarged heart and an intact sense of humor. As Ross Gay notes, "What if we joined our sorrows, and what if that is joy?"

I started living in the gap, the space between past and future because that's all we have. It squeezes between our two constants, life and death. It's finite, but, as Einstein discovered, time is relative because when you're living in the gap, time expands and constricts depending on the density of the moment. Falling in love, waiting for test results, standing in line at the DMV, watching a sunset, enduring a colonoscopy, or holding your newborn baby, these moments bend the arc of time, and that's the long and short of it.

My generation had a ton of mobility but no maps. It was like finding our way through a dark room, but we were unfamiliar with placing the furniture, and we got bruised. The slogan *she can have it all* was a mask, for she can do it all. "I can bring home the bacon, fry it up in a pan, and never let you forget you're a man," was the Enjoli commercial that terrorized a generation of women.

Most of my peers went to college, fell in love, married, and had children, but I grew up in the suburbs, and we were spoon-fed this formula from birth.

I stayed home because we kept checking kids into the womb. After four, we closed the *penal* institution permanently. Nipped that one in the bud, if you get my drift? I was thirty-five years old, knee-deep in shitty diapers, as I watched my peers climb the corporate ladder.

What do you do when your window of opportunity seems to be closing baby by baby? You go to graduate school just as you're entering menopause. This is your window of opportunity, education, and somehow it was left open for me.

With most of the kids flying the coop, moving into their own lives, I was just finding mine amidst hot flashes and mood swings. I dusted off my critical thinking skills, learned the benefits of online search engines, and started writing twenty-page research papers on the probability of God. Ends up, there's a good chance She's still putzing around the garden, with absolutely no remorse about kicking us out!

I took a position with Notre Dame High School and nested there for more than a decade, parenting someone else's kids, but they paid me. Writing became a survival technique because living in your own skin is tricky.

And then we wrinkle.

When my sister Nancy decided it was time for me to take a leap of faith, I took up her dare and started publishing my work in a blog aptly titled *Living in the Gap*. After stumbling around in the dark for decades, I started learning the layout, and what writing does for me is to shed light on the obstacles, the things that trip you up. And guess what? We're all dealing with the same blood, shit, and tears.

One of my readers, Delene Waltrip, wrote me a note recently: "I love your blog and your musings. They are all so poignant and resonate deeply with me, especially during the last two years. I feel like you say things that are rolling around in my brain, but I haven't put into a coherent thought. Thanks for making me feel not so alone. I'm betting others might feel the same." I sat down and cried, not sniffles, full-on wailing because some people shape their words just so, and somehow they fill that empty space in our hearts. She helped me understand how difficult it is to go it alone in this world, especially when someone is constantly rearranging the furniture.

It was my readers who set me straight, the ones like me, straddling two centuries with no map. We're doing the best we can. We're just trying to raise the kids, get the dog to the vet, manage our work in and out of the home, take care of aging parents, spoil the grandkids, contemplate retirement, and figure out how the hell we like our coffee. Hardships come and go like jobs, marriages, and friendships, and we've been forced to make some exceptionally hard choices these last few years.

Who expected a pandemic, sheltering in place, mask mandates, working and learning via Zoom would leave us feeling so isolated and alone? But now we know we can make it through the dark times because we just did, and we did it without toilet paper.

Here's the dirty little secret. We can laugh. It's the most intimate thing we can do with our clothes on. It's a radical act in a stoic world, and I believe it is one of our greatest gifts.

I'm Living in the Gap, feathers ruffled, writing myself out of the tight spots. I'm not going to bloom where I'm planted, as St. Francis philosophized. I'm going to *Grow Damn It!* and shatter the pot.

PART I: FOUNDATIONAL

LIVING IN THE GAP

"Faith empowers you to bridge the gap between imagination and materialization."
–Gugu Mona

Living in the gap, the space between past and future is not an easy task. I can spend so much time redeveloping the past or worrying about the future that I lose sight of the present. As Seth Godin notes, "I'm pretty confident that when the Titanic went down, the deck chairs were clean and well-ordered. It's a shame no one noticed the iceberg." Just this morning, I have no idea why, but I was writing the first line of my obituary in my head while enjoying my morning coffee. Seems odd, but when you get to know me, it all makes sense.

I considered the sentimental thoughts that would make the final draft: *I admired the sense of peace I always felt in her presence,* or *Didn't she have a smile for everyone?* Then I start worrying about my past behavior, like yesterday when I was stomping my foot and cussing like a sailor. I blamed everyone for my lost hairbrush. An hour later, I found it in the refrigerator. It happens. Or, the other morning, when I spent an entire hour lamenting over an ongoing marital argument while lounging in bed, and ostensively glared at my husband because he walked across the room.

I come back to the present when I take a sip of cold coffee, and I'm forced to make a trip to the kitchen for a warm-up. That's when the blackbirds shooting the shit out on the front lawn catch my attention. It's a holiday weekend, and garbage pickup is delayed. *Ruffled feathers and endless squawking over a minor difficulty are typical of a crow's life.*

I lean back on the counter and realize that could be my line...

SHE TOLD ME I COULD FLY

*"The moment you doubt whether you can fly,
you cease forever to be able to do it."*
–J. M. Barrie

"One day, I had an idea." This is the first line of a little book my sister Nancy gave me for my birthday in May of 2015. It was written by Kobi Yamada and titled, *What do you do with an idea?* She gave me this gift because she believes in me. From my earliest memories, this woman has had my back, and she protects my dreams like a well-worn jockstrap (a misfit metaphor if there ever was one, but it refuses to leave).

Nancy is my only sibling. She lives seven miles away, door to door. We calculated it once for fun. She dragged me to a Feng Shui class a few years ago, and now she claims my Qi is off because my front door is improperly positioned.

Flamboyant and mildly quirky, she has a heart of gold, and I have shamelessly monopolized her patience and affection for over half a century. Just entering a room, Nancy can infuse the atmosphere with enormous compassion and discernible warmth. She is the hand I reach for when I am happy, bored, bitchy, or despondent. I know her grip is solid, and she will not let go.

I have to admit there is comfort in knowing at least one person in this world knows everything about me (the fraudulent weight listed on my driver's license, my secret infatuation with Donny Osmond, even the stash of chocolate kisses I keep hidden in a tampon box in my bathroom cupboard), and she still loves me without reserve. Hiding is impossible with Nancy because she knows my moves and sees the truth, often before it is apparent to me. This is the resiliency of sisterhood. And best of all, when I call her in the middle of the night because I can't sleep, she acts like this is normal.

The importance of this little book is almost too significant to describe. As I opened this exquisitely wrapped package, she sat me down and insisted I read it from beginning to end. Older sisters are bossy. After the first reading, I looked up. We didn't speak a word. She just gave me this brief nod, and I knew the depth of her fertile generosity. She was willing me to go forth with my work as a writer, but I was scared. I have all the normal fears around exposure and, despite behavior to the contrary, I have never wanted people to think I am crazy, off-kilter, or worse, full of rubbish.

She was begging me to jump!

I should add she doesn't have an impressive track record when asking me to jump. When she was six (beyond the age of reason), and I was four, she told me I could fly. I believed her and jumped off a shallow ledge, resulting in a nasty cut to my upper lip. I still have the scar to prove it. She insists the story is exaggerated, but you can understand my hesitancy when she says, "Jump." I managed to overlook the past, took a leap of faith, and started a damn blog.

My fingers were actually shaking when I hit the publish button for the first time. My husband immediately yelled from the office, "You misspelled corral." I almost fainted. Then he said, "No, no, it's right."

"I liked being with my idea. It made me feel more alive, like I could do anything. It encouraged me to think big… and then, to think bigger," writes Kobi Yamada. I blogged daily for the entire summer. It was my greatest joy and one hell of a disastrous chore. I lived in fear that I used up all my words, there were no more valid experiences to write about, and three people were still reading (Mom, Nancy, & Larry) out of pure obligation.

Yamada writes, "Then, one day, something amazing happened. My idea changed right before my eyes. It spread its wings, took flight, and burst into the sky." This happened when Krista Tippett tweeted, "I love your blog." The power of one's sister, by blood or by choice, is truly a blessing. The page views lit up like the Rockies during the summer of 2015, and, of course, I called Nancy to tell her about my new BFF. I think she's jealous. She said, "Is she bothering you?"

Love you, my fearless guardian angel, my sister, my friend.

HAPPY BIRTHDAY DADDY

*"I believe that what we become depends on what our fathers teach us at odd moments, when they aren't trying to teach us.
We are formed by little scraps of wisdom."*
–Umberto Eco

It's my father's birthday today. He passed away more than a decade ago, but I like to spend time sifting through my memories on the day he came into the world.

I remember observing my father from a distance the morning he was scheduled for bypass surgery back in September of 2002.

It is a chilly Northwestern morning as I watch him adjusting his suspenders in the bathroom mirror. He reaches up to smooth his unruly gray hair, and I am charmed by the familiar gesture. I consider my dad a handsome man with a mischievous disposition. He has a gregarious nature and could charm the skin off a damn snake if necessary, but I got his eyes, and I believe we view life through a similar lens. I call this the blessing of the second born. (My older sister got his organizational skills, of which he had absolutely none.)

I notice that life has chiseled away his youthful features, like the faces of Mount Rushmore. I marvel at this monumental man.

He catches my eye in the mirror's reflection, casually holding my gaze as a lifetime of knowing passes between us. He gives me a little wink, and I tear up unexpectedly. It feels like a band is squeezing my chest, and I'm finding it hard to breathe.

My sister Nancy hands me a Styrofoam cup of coffee. Breaking the spell, she says, "Come on, it's time to go."

Today, I am forever grateful that he was willing to risk death just to add a few more years to his life. I would give anything for one more day with you.

Happy birthday, Daddy.

AFTER YOU SAY I DO

"Longed for him. Got him. Shit."
–Margaret Atwood

We were married less than a year when Larry walked through the door of our small apartment in Beaverton, Oregon, and announced, "We're moving back to California. I quit my job. Start packing."

"Shouldn't we discuss this first?"

Oh, the hell with it, I wasn't sure what I thought about the pool freezing over in our complex or the nonstop rain, and I was sort of homesick. I started folding, wrapping, and stacking our life in cardboard boxes. That's when all our belongings fit in a U-Haul trailer and our need for stability was minimal.

It was the second anniversary when we realized we cared for each other even more than last year.

Three years in, we gave birth to our first child, a mini-me, and Julie Mae became our world. Larry presented me with a beautiful Lladro figurine, something he would repeat with the births of our successive children, and those figurines still live on the mantle in the family room, sparking joy in my heart whenever I pass but also reminding me of the portals we overcome.

I think it was the fourth year, right after our move to Kansas, when our beloved child split her chin open on the edge of the bathtub. When we were in the recovery room, I realized I was wearing a nightshirt covered in blood, no bra, and bright pink sweats, but we learned how unified we could be when our child was in distress. We cried. We held her. We spoke words of comfort, and we no longer cared if she slept with us for the rest of our lives.

Six months later, we welcomed our second beautiful baby into the world. Her name is Kelley Ann. There are two things we know for sure: they were sent here from heaven, and they're Daddy's little girls (Bob Carlisle adapted). We decided being parents was so damn hard, except for the butterfly kisses, morning snuggles, and the patter of little feet on the hardwood floor. My prayers were completely redirected. All I could feel was enormous gratitude and sheer exhaustion, but God had my back.

In year seven, we moved back to California. I was eight months pregnant, and four weeks after moving halfway across the country, we welcomed our third child into the family, Anthony Joseph. Our hearts were on fire, and although outnumbered, we learned to multitask. At this point in time, I had been pregnant or nursing for six years, hadn't slept through the night in ages, and really had no business driving.

We didn't get the seven-year itch. We got promoted. Larry moved from medical into high tech, and suddenly our lives were immeasurably easier. We installed a car phone, put up a play set in the backyard, and discovered fine wine. Our house and hearts may have been in full bloom, but now and then, the weeds took over. You know what I mean? Bad seeds get mixed in with the good. It happens.

Larry doused that shit with roundup.

I think it was the ten-year mark when I realized I could not change the dude I married. It was the same month all of our children came down with chickenpox, and suddenly his travel schedule was unusually packed.

Hallmark does not make a card for this type of occasion.

I called my Mom, "S.O.S. I'm sinking. Send in the fucking coast guard." She was on the next flight and walked in the door just as I was throwing a shoe at the traveler for no reason. She caught it midair. Damn handy woman.

It's not a moment I'm proud of, but I tell you this because I've learned it's okay to ask for help. As most of you know, I would rather pull my fingernails out one at a time than admit defeat, but as if a card game, you have to "... know when to hold 'em, know when to fold 'em, know when to walk away, and know when to run," screaming to your Mama.

We took our first vacation without the children during our tenth year. Mom flew in to guard the nest. I wrote out a complex daily schedule, loaded the refrigerator with food, and left the insurance cards on the counter. When we returned, everyone was alive. A taxi was waiting in the driveway.

She couldn't get on that return flight faster.

It was year twelve, let's call it the difficult year, when I realized I could survive just about anything, but not on my own. Our fourth child arrived, Dante Richard. Traveler dropped me off at the curb with the child still in the car seat. A sign on the front lawn welcomed the baby home, and he headed to the airport for a week-long business trip. I was trippin'.

But Mom was there waiting for me. She had the older children dressed in matching sibling shirts, and she recently swept the kitchen floor. For some reason, this made me inordinately happy, and I sat down in the living room and cried.

That night, without a single word, Mom heard my silent anguish, walked into the room, took the cranky baby out of my arms, and put me to bed. Then she crawled in next to me, rubbed my back while she rocked the baby in her other arm, and put us both to sleep. I would one day do this for my child, but this is how I learned, her hand on my back, her heart holding my son.

One evening around year thirteen, traveler called from a swanky bar in downtown Boston, "What did you do today?" I thought he was kidding. We have four kids, a dog, a cat, and high-maintenance fish. They all need to be fed, clothed, taxied all over town (except the fish), and he wants to know WHAT I DID TODAY? Yeah, I hung up on him.

I decided it was time to go on strike (I may have overreacted a tad), but there is nothing worse than a woman on a diet, premenstrual, and perimenopausal. The combination can be lethal, especially for husbands. The poor guy had no idea what sort of storm was brewing at home.

I did absolutely nothing for four days and could hardly wait for him to walk in the door. When he did, I was ready, a beer in hand (I never drink beer, but it was the perfect prop), Magnum P.I. on the television, children running amuck, with no surface in the house visible. In fact, we had to create a path in order to get around.

He stepped carefully over all the rubble, leaned in to give me a kiss, and without a word, rolled up his sleeves, and started cleaning. Thirty minutes in, I asked for a cold beer and if he could hold off vacuuming until the commercial break. He was ever so accommodating.

I married a good one.

As Madeleine L'Engle claims, "No long-term marriage is made easily, and there have been times when I've been so angry or so hurt that I thought my love would never recover. And then, in the midst of near despair, something has happened beneath the surface. A bright little flashing fish of hope has flicked silver fins and the water is bright and suddenly I am returned to a state of love again — till next time."

By year thirteen, we expanded the house. It was as if I could breathe again. This was a good year.

During years fifteen, sixteen, and seventeen, we had the time of our lives. Sporting events dominated the calendar. Our neighbor Brighton, Dante's buddy, moved in with us for about seven years, my fifth child. The teens took over the house. Messaging became a thing. The front yard looked like a used car lot. We needed more chaperones because preaching abstinence seemed futile, and as everyone was learning to master their own lives, I was learning to let go. It hurt like hell.

We survived. We thrived. We may have even matured.

One evening, I glanced around the patio. Gathered at our ample table were some of our closest friends. We commonly refer to them as the gang. Phyllis, Jill, Mary, Greg, Steve, and Jim were sipping wine, laughing, and singing along with the Eagles. It was a cool evening after a warm summer day. When Larry was turning on the patio heater, I remember catching his eye and smiling because we both knew the rarity of true friends. These were the ones who picked us up when life won the round, and they did it with such grace we hardly noticed.

I applied to graduate school somewhere around year twenty, got accepted, and even graduated, but more importantly, I developed my critical thinking skills and landed a day job with a paycheck. We rambled around the almost empty nest and deemed it as good. I think we started dating again. (Update: my sister just called. She wanted to know who the hell I was dating? Hello, each other!)

Our first trip to Europe with those same good friends marked our twenty-fifth year, and we got bit hard by the travel bug. Italy rocks. I decided I didn't want to change him after all, and we both became frequent flyers.

Year twenty-seven, we lost my dad to an array of health issues. I had to learn to live with a gaping hole in my heart. I felt rudderless, so I just gave in to the waves of misery, and we learned how grief ebbs and flows, but also how to value the rapidly dwindling years.

Before long, daughter number one married the love of her life, Nic Jensen. We gained an incredible new son-in-law. On the morning of their wedding, Larry handed me a gift with my coffee. I said, "What in the world is this?" It was a Lladro, something to mark this momentous occasion, just like he did after the births of all our children. I sat in bed with this little boy figurine in my hand and cried. He so gets me.

By year twenty-eight, we bought a lake house in a desperate attempt to bring the family into one zip code. A place we could call our own, a way to stack up memories as if logs on a fire and hope those embers would keep us warm in the winter of our life.

By the way, we're toasty.

Was it year thirty when one of our children decided to move to Australia? He took a piece of my heart with him. I had to stop myself from chasing his taxi down the street. I hate goodbyes. There, I said it.

I'm still waiting for him to come home, but slowly learning home is where he makes it. I've had to let go of the idea that home was exclusively my place. Tissue, please.

Less than a year later, we welcomed our first grandchild, Audrey Mae, into the family, and our hearts grew three sizes that day. She lit up our world as if the fourth of July. We looked at each other with fresh eyes. We saw how love inflates, stretches, and repurposes everything we know to be rare and true. "To be fully seen by somebody, then, and be loved anyhow—this is a human offering that can border on miraculous," says Elizabeth Gilbert.

Somewhere during year thirty-two, twin granddaughters came into our lives, Cora Lynn and Sienna Jessica. It is not possible to understand how they doubled our joy, and just when I was learning to tell them apart, my beloved mother went off to be with dad. Did I mention I hate goodbyes?

Larry was my rock, but the pain of severing the umbilical cord from mother to child is unbearable. Nancy, my beloved sister, and I clung to each other as if our life depended on it. As it turns out, it did.

And we clung all the more when her husband lost his battle with diabetes, left us in the middle of the night, and suddenly my sister became a widow. There are no words at a time like this, just presence, tears, and love. The family flooded in, as did friends and neighbors, a beautiful tribute to the way David loved the people in his life. He would have said, "It's all good," because early on, he learned to trust in something much bigger than himself.

Life, ever a mixture of devastation and delight, set us off in celebration of daughter number two, who said yes to the ring last February, and Tim Bontemps finally joined the family slack channel. We looked at each other on our second flight out to Boston in one week, my foot still in a boot, and deemed ourselves ever so lucky. My soon-to-be son-in-law pulled everything off without a hitch. Love is in the air...

I think it was year thirty-six when we bought each other cards and forgot to give them to each other. It's the thought that counts. As Dave Meurer claims, "A great marriage is not when the 'perfect couple' comes together. It is when an imperfect couple learns to enjoy their differences."

The things we have collected over the years no longer fit in a U-Haul, but the things that matter do not take space, money, or go on strike. I've learned that real love forces you to weed out the rubbish and embrace the good in each other because, as we know, love is patient, love is kind. It does not envy, it does not boast, it is not proud. It does not dishonor others, it is not self-seeking, it is not easily angered, it keeps no record of wrongs. Love does not delight in evil but rejoices with the truth. It always protects, always trusts always hopes, always perseveres, as if figurines on a mantel, sparking joy in the lives of our beloved. (Adapted 1 Corinthians)

I still love watching him walk into a room. I love when he pulls me into a warm embrace and when he kisses me slowly. Kahlil Gibran notes love is "...to melt and be like a running brook that sings its melody to the night. To know the pain of too much tenderness. To be wounded by your own understanding of love; And to bleed willingly and joyfully."

This is what happens after you say, "I do.

THIS IS A WOMAN TO LOVE

"That it will never come again is what makes life so sweet."
–Emily Dickinson

She might be small in stature, but this woman is large in life. One who is quiet by nature, always on the go, annoyingly optimistic, but never a pushover. She can be obliging, but if you walk on her freshly mopped floors, she will take you down. Seriously, she has an adorable laugh, holds my secrets like a priest, and showers me with undeserved compassion rather than judgment.

She is my dream come true. My first mentor. Directly responsible for my annoying optimism, organizational skills, and ability to read. I have observed her so closely through the years that I do not know where she ends, and I begin. Sometimes I catch myself speaking her words, words I swore I would never verbalize, and it makes me laugh.

I watch my hands move in the same patterns when nervous, and on any given day, I would prefer an old movie, popcorn, and soda over the social scene.

Can I just add, living with a bunch of introverts is exhausting. When mom needed a cup of sugar from the neighbor, she sent me. When someone called for a toast, a speech, or a narrator, I was gently pushed front and center. This is how they tried to convince me I was an extrovert so they could all stay home and read.

It's as if I was born left-handed, and they forced me to do everything with my right. I'm what you call a forced extrovert with an ambidextrous personality disorder. And by the way, the right never knows what the hell the left is doing.

Truthfully, they thought I was amalgamation gone wrong. Mom threw her Dr. Spock book in the garbage when I came along, and now she describes me as her "active" child. Love her.

I marvel at the virtue of adaptability this woman modeled through the years. She grew up in the Bay Area, met her lifelong sweetheart on the campus of Los Gatos High School, and graduated from San Jose State with a teaching credential.

The apple doesn't fall far from the tree.

Larry and I met at Del Mar High School, and although he did not know it at the time, a decade later, I'd be adopting his name. He drove a newly refurbished Nova, and I believe I procured the first kiss, but he came back for seconds.

Mom was a product of her time and took on the traditional roles in our household. Just about every morning she'd be in the kitchen, in her bathrobe, frying up bacon and eggs, pouring us coffee before we clamored out the door. I used to think poor woman, she must sit home all day waiting for us to return, because I always found her in the kitchen ready to listen to our stories and provide a snack when I walked in the door. Little did I know the minute we left the house she whipped off that housecoat, slipped into a swanky tennis outfit, and she was off to the courts. Mom was active before active was cool. In 1974, when girls were allowed to compete in after school sports, she championed my involvement. Or she was simply thrilled to have found an ally in helping to burn off my energy.

I remember the day mom and dad announced they were relocating to the Northwest. At nineteen, I was all set to attend San Jose State in the fall.

Nancy had just returned from the Fashion Institute in Los Angeles and would finish her bachelor's at SJSU.

Mom was anguishing in her room about the unexpected move while Nancy and I were sobbing on the couch, with my poor dad struggling to bridge the gap. The good news is mom survived, and even though it was a brutal adjustment, she persevered through the rough spots, kept her anguish to herself, and as always, made the best of a difficult situation. This is my legacy, and I am forever grateful she is the success story I am privileged to emulate.

In recent years, I watched my mom go to battle with the spirit of death for my dad, and with the last of her strength, she held that spirit at bay, but when it was time, she had the grace to let him go.

She struggled with her new status as a widow, but again, I marveled at her resilience. There we were, three women adrift at sea, brutally detached from our beloved anchor. Nancy and I watched in horror as mom struggled in the raging water then, with unheard of strength, she swam towards us, wrapped us in her arms, and we were able to form a small buoy of our own. Like Molly Brown, she showed us how to survive a tragedy in the midst of her own.

We will never be the same without our dad, and I know this is the most difficult passage of her life. She combats loneliness with an active schedule. She lapses, prevails, and had to learn to do things on her own. Mom quickly discovered the protection of old friends (you all know who you are, and we thank you), she kept moving, and made the courageous decision not only to live but to live well. This is one of the best gifts she has bestowed on me since the day I was born.

This is a woman to love.

This is my mama.

THE FAMILY TREE

"I stored all our memories in this tree."
–Santosh Kalwar

The rings of thoughts circling my mind have taken a detour as I rest in the shade of wisdom. I'm a bit of an emotional wreck. I sit in my backyard, commiserating with my beautiful magnolia tree, deeply rooted in the western corner. This is the space I return to, time after time, to think, to lament, to listen.

Today I seek the soothing presence of my beloved tree, who assures me, "All is well. All is well. All is well."

When I consider the layers of stories this tree has witnessed, I dissolve into her past, viewing life from a loftier perspective. I believe she found fertile ground before the neighborhood was conceived. She started her life amid a prune orchard, wide open and free.

When the contractors marched onto her land, the ground was subdivided, and foundations were laid. Families in search of shelter formed a simple but solid community. She knew who my good friends would be before I did. She enticed them into the neighborhood so they would find me.

This tree watched over me in grade school as I roamed the streets at midnight, accompanied by a gaggle of silly girlfriends armed with stolen toilet paper and mischievous intentions. We would decorate the houses of the boys we liked with our long white streamers, then run squealing back to the safety of our family room, sleeping bags, and youthful camaraderie.

We were spoiled, naïve, and innocent, but the tree knew better.

Magnolia was part of my childish dreams, my secrets still deeply rooted in her soil, permanently stored in her rings of knowledge. This tree lived a few blocks away from my family home, but her tall branches kept me in view. She stood silent, stoic, a sentinel in the night. Like the world, she, too, has experienced periods of creation and destruction.

A witness to generations of trick-or-treaters, neighborhood parades, and family celebrations, but also death, sickness, and the dismantling of families. As our lives branched out into the world, so did our tree.

I left the neighborhood for a while, ran off with the boy I loved, and lived as far away as Kansas, but the tree never forgot me. When she called me home, I came running. We bought the house with my beloved tree in 1990, and four weeks later, we brought home our third child, a baby boy named Anthony Joseph Oreglia.

She is not a neutral member of our family. She is a noble witness, alive and vital, but rarely paid homage. This tree has hidden Easter eggs, been our safe base for freeze tag, shaded our playhouse, and become our centurion during backyard campouts. I have turned to her trusted presence for most of my life.

We had to cut off one of her branches when we were expanding our nest. She didn't make a sound, but I know we wounded her.

She was a Christmas present one year, as we built a fort in her sturdy branches, and this shelter became my children's refuge for fifteen years. They carved the names of their loved ones in her branches. She shaded tables at graduations, birthdays, and holidays.

Our tree has joined us for numerous dinner parties as we sit beneath her majestic branches, our voices drifting into the wee hours of the night. She is as familiar as a wine glass in the hands of our friends, embedded in our memories, her presence invaluable.

I am a little nostalgic today as my son Tony prepares for an extended journey. He will be living in Australia for the next year and a half. I cannot really think about his departure without tearing up and losing my composure, so I ignore the calendar and the shrinking days to this arduous goodbye.

He will grow as a man during this time. He will have many experiences that I will not witness, and this causes an ache deep in my heart. I trust this young man to direct his own life, seek out new challenges, and follow his own destiny. He is ever so compassionate, capable, and strong. I will miss him more than he will ever know.

I worry that our family cat will have passed before he returns. In two years, he might have a new niece or nephew to love. I will miss his passion for life, his noble influence in our home, and our early morning chats over coffee. Tony has grown up in this house. There is not a place I can turn where the memory of my son doesn't come to mind.

It was our beloved tree who watched in horror as this young man mounted his bicycle in our driveway, rode through an occupy rally in Oakland, crossed the Carquinez Bridge, and climbed the Mayacamas Mountains by moonlight, ending up in Clearlake after a twenty-three-hour solo ride. No one knew but the tree. He has an adventurous spirit that will not be tamed.

I sit quietly beneath the family tree, silent, strong, and centered. I hear her whisper in the breeze, "All is well. All is well. All is well."

MY DAUGHTER SHOWS UP AT THE HOUSE WITH TWO DEAD FISH

"She did not stand alone, but what stood behind her, the most potent moral force in her life, was the love of her father."
–Harper Lee

It's 9 a.m. when my daughter Kelley shows up at the house with two dead fish. She has a detailed plan for our Father's Day meal. I am selected from a wide pool of possibilities to be a sous chef and financier. Okay, the truth is, no one else wanted the jobs.

She has a stack of recipe books with numerous pages tagged, and we have a slew of instructional videos at our fingertips. I hyperventilate because elaborate recipes are not my thing. Our first task is to create a grocery list, then we set off to Lundardi's market in search of fresh ingredients. Seriously, hours later, we arrive back at the house with four bags of groceries and an abridged bank account. No rhubarb was to be found, but they had everything else.

Kelley slaps on an apron and gets to work. I'll just say it: within the space of an hour, my kitchen is in agony (or maybe that was me). Tidiness is not her superpower.

Spices, bowls, measuring cups, pans, rolling pins, pots, spatulas, knives, and cutting boards literally cover every conceivable space. I am finding it hard to breathe.

She has the bourbon-glazed pork belly and the St. Louis ribs all prepared for three hours of slow cooking. I tucked the pie crust dough in the refrigerator. The black beans are low boiling on the stove. I'm engaging in positive self-talk about the mess and the twelve people who will be arriving soon.

This is when I recognize the benefits of resiliency. See, we had a power surge the day before, and unbeknownst to me, it took out our oven. It is dead, dark, and cold, refusing to come back to life. Yes, I resorted to prayer, but Jesus was not available (Father's Day and all), so with my cell phone in hand, I'm ready to call out for pizza.

Kelley says, "mom, calm down, we'll cook the meat at Julie's house. I'll call Ron and Debbie (our beloved neighbors) and see if we can use their oven to cook the pies."

What?

I am a zero at adaptability and I think we should seriously reschedule Father's Day.

A few phone calls later, she calmly arranged for the use of several ovens. She packs up the meats and escorts me to the car before I can run screaming down the street. I'll be damned if it doesn't all work out. On our way home, we try one more store for the rhubarb — success!

Back at the house, we prepare the grilled artichokes, stuffed tilapia, blue cheese wedge salads, and pies. I'm setting tables and washing dishes while simultaneously working on my blog and let me just say the blog is losing. The wines are breathing much better than I am when the guests arrive. I decide to just let the kitchen go and enjoy the evening.

It is magical, from the Bourbon-glazed pork belly appetizer to the stuffed tilapia, wedge salads, grilled artichokes, St. Louis barbecue ribs, Cuban-style black beans, and homemade pies. The table goes completely silent. Mere words are inadequate. This is our thanks and praise to Kelley.

My husband is so happy he breaks open a bottle of Darioush Cabernet Sauvignon to accompany our meal. Kelley is a rock star.

After dinner, I slip away into my room with my granddaughter Audrey, and we curl up in bed. We are both exhausted. I whisper stories in her ear as her eyes slowly close, and she sleeps in the crook of my arm.

As I listen to the voices coming from the patio, I realize this is an extraordinary moment—makes me tear up just thinking about it. Here we are celebrating a good man with an extraordinary meal, and all my kids are gathered around one table. It doesn't get better than this.

CLEARLAKE
THE MOORING OF A FAMILY

"Looking out over the lake, I felt enveloped in the most peaceful, loving utopia."
–Laurie Kahn

Rising early from my warm bed, where sleep has been evasive, I grab an old sweatshirt and make my way to the living room. I notice the lake is completely hidden by a fog bank, the density so thick my eyes cannot penetrate. The sun is about to clear the horizon, and for some reason, the world is presenting itself in layers of light, brume, and murky darkness, as if delineating heaven and hell on this sentient canvas.

As I stand here, a curious thing happens. The fog begins to lift as if the parting of a curtain, and this tiny revelation takes my breath away.

I really need some coffee, don't you think?

We purchased the Clearlake house over a decade ago, our children were still in their teens, and we've never regretted this monumental decision. Not even when we found a snake in the house or a gigantic spiker living in my closet. I have yet to tire of this view, and my gratitude bubbles over as if my soul were a flute of fine champagne.

Living by the lush landscapes of Clearlake, if only on the weekends, is enormously conducive to human thriving. The landscape has *driven deep grooves into my psyche* (a Robert Macfarlaneism), and I am forever entangled in her unique wisdom. I find it interesting that landscapes can have such a significant impact on our well-being.

The lake doesn't just surround me; it becomes me.

She elevates my thoughts and drags me again and again to my computer in an attempt to capture this intangible love affair, but words defy the depth of our relationship. *She expands my range of thought, and when I think of this in human terms, this is probably the most beautiful thing we can do for each other.*

Clear Lake is a natural freshwater lake in Lake County, just forty miles north of Napa and San Francisco. It is the largest natural freshwater lake in California. At an age of 2.5 million years, it is the oldest lake in North America, and, might I add, it is nice not being the oldest presence in the room.

She's a survivor by design. The lake sits on a huge block of stone which slowly tilts northward at the same rate as the lake fills in with sediment, thus keeping the water at roughly the same depth year after year.

Our home is part of the Kono Tayee Estates, which sounds fancy, but it's simply a peninsula of land on the East shore, which was subdivided in the 50s by a developer who sold the lots individually. My husband's father bought one of the last lots in the 70s and built a home for his family. We purchased our house on the other side of the subdivision in 2010; it's Mediterranean style, with stucco walls and a red tiled roof, which suits us just fine.

We had no grandchildren at the time of purchase; none of our children were even married, but I visualized the family's expansion, and this house has graciously accommodated our every need. Two sons-in-law have since joined the family, along with three adorable grandchildren. Our precious Shaggy dog has come and gone, but I'm not done visualizing by any stretch of the imagination.

While we were visiting Tony and Thalita in Portugal last year, we purchased handmade tiles with the Oreglia family name painted in bold letters surrounded by grape leaves. Larry embedded the tiles into the stucco wall to the left of the front door, and it's as if our name has always graced the courtyard wall.

Precious memories have become so entwined with the lake that it's hard to imagine this property falling into anyone else's hands. Regardless, it will now permanently bear our family name.

Although this is one of my favorite places to write, conspire, and allow my tightly wound world to unfurl, Lake County has many things to see and do. From water sports to fine dining, antiquing and wine tasting, kayaking, and hiking. I should really be the president of the tourist board.

And let me just say if you get bored at the lake, that's on you.

As luck would have it, the wine industry discovered our hidden jewel decades ago, and coincidentally, the soil around the lake is complementary to a variety of grapes. Over the years, several extraordinary wineries have opened tasting rooms in Lake County. We're all about supporting the local businesses, so we joined at least half a dozen wine clubs, and I admit we frequent these quaint establishments whenever possible. [*see Notes Lake County Wineries]

Slipping into a comfy deck chair, I rest my bare feet on the railing and watch the sun playing peek-a-boo with the horizon. I notice the last of the bats are returning home after a satisfying night of scavenging bugs, and at least a dozen Canadian Geese curled up on the beach's edge as if an extravagant pie crust. The sound of the water lapping against the shore is so soothing despite an aggressive crow who has repeatedly tried to gain access to a flight of swallows that have taken refuge under the neighbor's boathouse. I watch with amusement as three or four of the males chase him away.

It's a menagerie of continual movement, yet I sit motionless, mesmerized by the prehistoric feel of this rustic scene playing out before my eyes. This is our sacred space. I like to think of it as a *thin place* where the veil between heaven and earth is most transparent. I hold not a worry on my mind but a cup of warm coffee in my hand and a heart full of gratitude.

HE HAD ME AT "A ROUNDED SUBSTANTIAL BECOMING"

"One of the deepest longings of the human soul is to be seen."
–John O'Donohue

John O'Donohue says that God is beauty. Not the beauty you see splashed across the pages of a glamour magazine, but beauty "as a rounded substantial becoming, as an emerging fullness, a greater sense of grace and elegance, a deeper sense of depth, and also a kind of homecoming for the enriched memory of your unfolding life."

My God, who speaks like that?

He had me at "a rounded substantial becoming." I was listening to John in one of his last interviews with Krista Tippett before his unexpected death in 2008. I had to pause the conversation several times to listen deeply before I was able to soak up his words as if a dry sponge. He is magnetizing, and Tippett stays right with him, directing, pushing, and asking for more.

Krista Tippett says, "O'Donohue understands beauty as a human calling and a defining aspect of God." He tries to help us understand the working of our invisible world, those hidden aspects of self, some of which we will never fully understand. He says poetry, drama, dance, music, and art are forms that try to make the invisible concrete.

I so agree. I am thankful for people who dig deep within themselves and are able to reveal a universal aspect of the world through art. I've been brought to tears by a poignant Cappella. I've seen an entire room silenced by a good poem, and I think dance can be a mime of the soul.

He said, "Music is what language would be if it could." I also love the emphasis he puts on the landscape. O'Donohue is aware that our surroundings have a tremendous influence on our inner selves, and he believes it is how we stay in rhythm with the universe. He claims we could learn a lot if we walked outside every morning and realized the environment is alive. O'Donohue advises us to keep an image of nature tucked away in the mind like a picture of a loved one. The sun rising over my beloved Clearlake is the image I have stored away. I retrieve it when I need a refreshing calm.

O'Donohue says we are strangers to ourselves and collapsing under the burden of stress. He encourages us to see the beauty in our friendships. Our most intimate relationships are truly an aspect of the divine. These are the people who love us deeply, who remind us of our goodness, and who help us to become our best selves. We should surround ourselves with those who hold us dear. I think we awaken the best or worst in each other through the fruition of our inner selves. This is our well, and this is all we have to offer. It is so simple.

Our fast-moving culture doesn't allow us the space to fully unfold to develop important friendships, and we've replaced our ability for an honest conversation with text messages and email. I have a small dinner party planned for tomorrow night with the usual suspects, and I can't wait to tell each of them how important they are to me. He reminds us it is not until we are on the verge of losing someone that we understand their deep relevance. The blatant truth changes us and pushes us towards a more authentic self. I am grateful Tippett was able to immortalize O'Donohue's words in this powerful interview.

I am on fire with this man's wisdom. O'Donohue speaks of God, like Cruise to Zellweger, "You complete me." He's written several books, a national bestseller called *Anam Cara*, which means soul friend, and a more recent work called *Divine Beauty*. He says, "The glory of God is the human person fully alive." Hallelujah! I just put my order in with Amazon. Let's hope the drone can find me.

[This is the blog that Krista Tippett noted in a tweet. She linked it to her Twitter account and went on sabbatical for a month. Her generosity changed my life.]

PART II: TRANSITIONAL

TRUE GRIT

"Do not let temporary setbacks become permanent excuses."
–**Angela Duckworth**

I'm so mesmerized by the view of the lake I can't seem to focus on what I'm doing, and believe me, this has dire consequences. Yesterday I spent two hours working on a new blog. I'm sure it was epic. Apparently, I saved it incorrectly, and it disappeared like dark chocolate and red wine.

Total fail.

I spent another hour messing around with the history link, to no avail. Screw the past. The blog was about memory and how it retires around the same time we do. The irony of losing my memory along with my blog is not lost on me. I just don't find it amusing.

I remember hosting a dinner party when I was in my mid-forties. There were eight of us sitting around the patio late one evening and sipping wine. We were discussing an old movie with John Wayne and a snake pit, but none of us could remember the title (this was the pre-smartphone era).

"It had something to do with sand?"

"It was one word, or maybe two?"

"Rhymes with pit?"

I woke up in the middle of the night yelling, "True Grit, True Grit." Larry thought I was having a nightmare. He started shaking me, "Honey, wake up, wake up." I sat straight up in bed. "Stop shaking me. I'm having an epiphany, not a bad dream. Open some damn champagne."

The point I'm trying to make is memory loss was happening all along. This isn't something new. The dinner party was proof, but back then, I knew the information would eventually resurface. Now I think my memories are lying dormant in some inescapable brain pit surrounded by snakes.

I'm totally dependent on my smartphone. I wonder if this is slowly changing my ability to memorize information. Google has become my offsite memory source. What is the fallout from this metaphysical shift? Hold on... I'll google it.

It's called nomophobia, the fear of being without your smartphone, and I learned it affects forty percent of the population. People afflicted with this phobia become dysfunctional when separated from their phones. But I digress, so I closed the damn computer and told Larry, "Ditch the sweats, Honey. We're going wine tasting, and you're buying me a picnic lunch."

I gave him the don't mess with me look, which never works. "I'm watching the game, and the refrigerator is full of food," he quips.

Walking over to mute the television, I say, "I'm leaving in ten minutes, with or without you." I rubbed some sunscreen on my face and slapped on earrings, jeans, and a baseball hat. Then, I stood by the front door, stomping my foot, "I'm going..."

He's still lounging on the couch. He takes a minute to size me up and decides a glass of wine might be an amicable solution, or he likes my tight jeans (I eat too much, but that's beside the point). Eventually, he complies.

We reach the top of the hill at Kono Tayee, and he says, "Where're we going?"

I'm feeling generous. "I'll let you decide."

We land at Cashe Creek Winery, located off Highway 20. It has a welcoming venue. The building is circular, made of refurbished wood from an old water tower. We're members here, so they know us, and everything we buy is discounted. Most things are overpriced to begin with, so it's always helpful to belong.

We are the only customers, and the hostess is generous with the pours. We sit outside with our salami-wrapped cheese sticks (this is what Larry considers a picnic) and glasses of wine.

I whine, "I can't believe I lost an entire morning's work."

"Recreate it."

"I'll never remember it all."

"Tough times don't last. Tough people do." (Larry's go-to philosophy for every hardship in life)

"That makes me feel so much better." I want to splash a little wine in his face, but that would be a waste of good wine.

Life rarely goes the way I plan, but most of the time, giving up is not an option. This is where true grit comes into play (passion and perseverance for long-term goals, as Angela Duckworth notes), and this happens to be the most significant predictor of success for individuals. Not intelligence, talent, or memory, but grit.

Grit grows as we age like our noses and ears. Every time we pick ourselves off the floor and start again is a testament to this developing skill. Learning to discern between what is necessary and what is optional allows us to focus on what matters most as we age.

Persevering after failure is learned behavior, and it is the one damn thing that improves with age! Booya! OMG, failure is not a permanent condition. This must be true, or you wouldn't be reading this essay.

25 THINGS I WISH I HAD ASKED MY PARENTS

"In wondering bout the big things and asking bout the big things, you learn about the little ones, almost by accident. The more I wonder, the more I love."
–Alice Walker

It's mid-morning. I'm lounging on my sister's couch. We're sipping coffee, shooting the shit, and verbally redecorating her guest room from our prone positions.

Out of the blue, she says to me, "I wish I had asked mom about death."

I say, "Do you mean how she felt about dying?"

"No, how she managed after dad died."

"That would have been good to know."

"I was afraid to ask. I thought it might be too difficult for her to talk about, so I avoided the subject."

"I believe it was the most challenging thing she ever had to deal with."

"I know."

"I know you know." (My sister's beloved husband passed away unexpectedly in the middle of the night.)

This, of course, got me thinking about the things I wish I had asked my parents before they passed. Things Nancy and I are left to piece together from separate conversations, but that will never be the same as an intentional discussion while your parents are alive and able to articulate their own thoughts.

So, I started thinking about some things my parents went to their graves without telling us. Things I wish I knew more about because they could have informed my life today or at least given me a more detailed picture of the people who brought me into the world. If you still can talk with your parents, then do so before it's too late. Here is a mixture of questions I've asked my parents over the years and a few things I remain curious about, but no longer have a chance to discuss with them.

This list is far from complete, but it's a start, questions to leisurely discuss with your loved ones and a way of reminiscing together and sharing your stories.

Get the nitty, gritty details about their childhood?
1. What is one of your best childhood memories? I want the long version, no detail is unimportant.
2. Tell me about growing up in your hometown. What neighbors did you love? Who was the most scandalous or annoying? Who kept your secrets?
3. Tell me a favorite story about your mom and dad (my grandparents) or maybe something they wouldn't want me to know. Yes, I'm malicious. Don't let that stop you.

What did adulting look like in their day?
1. What was it like to live during [fill in the blank] World War II, the civil rights movement, the sexual revolution, women's liberation, Watergate, Woodstock, Neil Armstrong, cocktail parties where the martinis were shaken, not stirred?

2. How did you meet each other? Who initiated the first kiss? Who said "I love you" first? When did you decide to marry? And don't leave out a single detail about the proposal. I want all of it: what was said, where you were, how it felt, who you told!
3. What was your greatest fear about becoming a parent? I realize Dr. Spock was a heavy influence but give me some of your hard-earned parenting advice.
4. What is your best memory of me? Okay, and the worst? Try to be gentle.
5. What "tested your mettle" in this life, and what did you learn about yourself?
6. If you could change one thing about your life, what would it be? Be daring with this one, wishing you were taller doesn't count, but occupations, mistakes, and challenges do.
7. What do you love most about your spouse? I remember my mom telling me that dad made her a better person, and I believe that is about the best compliment you could give someone.
8. Are there any dreams you still might want to fulfill in this life, living in Paris for a year, joining the Peace Corps, or taking up ballroom dancing?
9. Or are you content with this life? No points for hiding behind the truth!
10. What advice would you give your fifty-year-old self? And do you mind if I record this part?
11. What are the three best decisions you've ever made? The worst? If need be, you can take the fifth, but what fun is that?
12. Aside from me, what are you most proud of in this life?
13. What event/s most profoundly shaped your life in good ways and bad?
14. Any important messages for your grandchildren?

Thoughts about God, misgivings, and general survival techniques?
1. Let's not talk about hell and damnation, but what about salvation, eternal life, and heaven? Your thoughts? Try to be honest instead of profound.
2. Tell me a secret you've told no one. I won't judge. I won't comment. I won't tell... I'll just hold it for you so you can let it go.
3. In three words, how do you want to be remembered? Hot, sassy, and

intelligent are already taken.
4. In practical terms, how do you survive the death of a spouse? Tom Hanks said, "I'm gonna get out of bed every morning... breath in and out all day long. Then, after a while, I won't have to remind myself to get out of bed every morning and breathe in and out... and, then after a while, I won't have to think about how I had it great and perfect for a while."
5. Are you scared of death? I read somewhere that death is like standing on the edge of the Grand Canyon. It's so much more than you could have imagined, and the view does not disappoint.
6. What will you miss? (This is a Nora Ephron question.) Because aside from my husband, six kids, and three grandchildren, I'll miss bacon, twinkle lights, the lake house, and let's not forget Amazon.com.

Don't forget the practical stuff because it will make life a lot easier when the time comes.
1. Do you have your affairs in order? What do I need to know?
2. How do you want your life to be celebrated?
3. What do you want to be done with your remains? I need specifics because otherwise, you'll end up in an urn at the lake house mixed in with a menagerie of distant relatives.

If I had the chance to do it all again, I would have disregarded my fear of resurrecting deeply suppressed emotions and asked, anyway. If we fail to acknowledge what we have here and now, it might be too late, and the opportunity will have passed. I would have said again and again how much I love them, how grateful I am to have them as my parents, and how enormous my gratitude is for the time we've had together.

It takes honesty and courage to face our lives, and consider what we've brought into this world, be it positive or negative. None of these questions are easy. Just try and answer a few for yourself. The most positive aspect of death, if there is one, tells us not to waste time but to love one another.

I wish I had recorded my mom reading to her great-granddaughter. I wish I knew how much I would miss my mom and dad before they parted. I wish I had spent more time in meaningful conversation because I truly believe understanding the endless array of human experience from my parents' perspective is key to unlocking the mysteries in my own life.

As Tolkien claims, "… the journey doesn't end here. Death is just another path. One that we all must take." Plato says, "Let parents bequeath to their children not riches, but the spirit of reverence." I say bequeath your story because even though part of us died with the passing of each parent, we are guardians of their legacy and, therefore, we'll never be alone. I liken death to a form of liberty, freedom from the bonds of this physical world, a bondage necessary for love to reign.

MIDLIFE, NETTLES, AND ROCKING CHAIRS

"When I'm 80 and sitting in a rocking chair listening to the Rolling Stones, there is absolutely no way I'm going to feel old or forget my younger days."
–Patty Duke

It's dusk. I'm rocking two naked grandbabies in an oversized nursery room rocker. They are not only identical, but perfectly replicate my memories of motherhood, including the exhaustion, multitasking, and rituals to release the daily burdens.

Not that you asked, but here's what I've been thinking...

I'm sensitive, hypersensitive, if you will, but that's the way I came into the world, and there is not much I can do about it. This sensitivity I speak of is a double-edged sword because not only am I sensitive in a normal sort of way, one who wears her feelings on her sleeve, but also inversely, which includes the rather nettlesome ability to feel the emotional energy of others. Most people come wired this way. Some seem more cognizant than others, but that's irrelevant.

Have you ever run your hand over a prickly cactus and for days been tortured by the tiny nettles that became embedded in your skin, invisible to the eye but distressing nonetheless? That outer layer of skin, known as the epidermis, as in you're getting under my skin, dude, and I'm feeling nettled! It's as aggravating as it is painful, and unless you're prepared to pluck them out one by one with a magnifying glass, you'll have to remember which cacti should be avoided and which are harmless, same with people.

You know what I'm talking about? When you feel pricked by the tiny, sharp, poignant feelings of those around you, as if you were a human pin cushion, and the only way to survive these porcupinian encounters is to retreat to a safe corner and write.

Perhaps this is why stories have unguent properties as if a healing salve? They anoint, consecrate, and possibly ordain our hallowed lives with an inviolable purpose, one that has the ability to calm irritations and rash behavior.

Don Miguel Ruiz wrote a book called *The Four Agreements*, and I think he nails the meddlesome game. Ruiz reminds us to be impeccable with our words, not to take anything personally or make assumptions, and always do our best. In doing so, we release our emotional cache. We become unencumbered, liberated, and immunized from the sting of intuitive encounters. This is a skill. It's learned behavior. Over time, it becomes a habit, which eventually informs our character.

I'm a bit of a sloth emotionally, but progress is relative, and please try to resist calculating my operatic health as I share a recent experience that tested my mettle. I took an early morning call from Julie, who asked me to accompany her to the elementary school this evening for the annual book fair and ice cream social with three of my favorite granddaughters. You don't have to ask me twice.

It starts at 5:30 p.m., so I drive straight to Julie's from work, entering the kitchen with a gregarious hello, scrambling from child to child for kisses. This is when I notice all the seismic activity going on in the room. Translation: everyone is on a sugar low, highly sensitive, and plying for Mom's attention.

Julie moves from one child to the next with the practiced grace of a prima ballerina, minus the tutu. She's soothing, calming, and nurturing, whereas I'm compelled to rummage through the refrigerator in search of cheese, peanut butter, or yogurt, anything that will ease this precipitous hunger. I also have a distinct feeling that I need to cry.

I'm doing my best to hold it together with these wigged-out miniature humans, shoveling Cheez-Its dipped in peanut butter into their birdlike mouths, and by the grace of God, when their deprived systems recover, I actually feel the atmosphere in the room shift. We haven't left the house, and yet I'm exhausted.

In need of a sedative for my sensitivities, I pour myself some blessed wine and find the search for matching shoes and socks slightly amusing.

Buckling all these kangaroos into the minivan is heroic. I'm just sayin'.

We arrive at the school and scamper to join the line forming by the cafeteria door. We are handed an empty bowl as we pass through the crowded portal. Servers are standing ready to place a scoop of ice cream in your bowl. There are two choices, chocolate or vanilla ice cream. Maybe a little of both? Who can deny adorable two-year-olds and their grey-haired Grammie? Volunteers, that's who, with no remorse or leniency. Move along. Move along.

Spread out on the cafeteria tables are large bowls of sprinkles, cans of whipped cream, and containers of chocolate sauce. Who thought this was a good idea? I don't mean to tattle, but some of the unsupervised children have weaponized these condiments, spraying unsuspecting souls with whipping cream, then sprinkling them with candy confetti. It's like being tossed in a paintball war with no barriers. I'm traumatized by the stickiness of it all, but try not to take it personally, as Ruiz warns, "It's not about you."

I forget how children are in constant motion. It's impossible to predict the calamity of encounters during these impromptu socials. Someone (I'll not mention names because I'm impeccable with my words) knocks over not only her own dish of ice cream but falls into the bowl of her neighbor. Somehow a spoon goes flying, which I'm able to grab midair, but this, of course, means my hand is now covered with a slimy film. And yes, my coat will need dry cleaning.

Julie's handing out baby wipes as if they were the solution to all our problems (not that I'm making assumptions). The children seem ignorant as to their genuine purpose, which is extracting gunk from their person. They start wiping down the cafeteria tables, Cinderella fashion, tossing the soiled clothes in the garbage, faces still covered in chocolate. I'm slightly appalled but doing my best to act nonplussed and, quite convincingly, I might add.

With the chaos of the room bearing down on me (I'm sensitive), we decide to move our slimy entourage to the book fair and out of the war zone.

I realize this event depends on the generous service of volunteers, but who decided to line the smallest of rooms imaginable with stacks of books, all within reach of children with severe ice cream hangovers, enabling them to grab and hoard? You can only imagine the mayhem.

There is crying, raging tantrums, and pulling of hair, but that's just me (doing my best). Haggard parents. Children screaming, "I want this, all of these, and I have to have the one with Elsa, please..." I count no less than twenty parents madly waving credit cards at the two volunteers as if trying to surrender after a lengthy battle. I just want to retreat and lick my wounds.

Did I mention it's smoldering hot in this little room? I'm stripping off layers of clothing as I work my way around the stacks of disarrayed books and try to keep an eye on our motley crew. They are darting around like little minions on steroids, and then there's Julie, calm as a Hindu cow, reading through the intros of several books, serenely discerning what she wants to buy. Really?

"Julie, for the love of God, let's get the hell out of here while there's still time!" People are staring at me as if I'm some kind of alarmist. I'm feeling so much desperation I can hardly breathe, and every Ruiz agreement went flying out the door.

For me, this is akin to falling in a vat of cacti, and as I'm gathering nettles under my skin, I somehow manage to buy forty dollars' worth of books.

Back at the house, we work as a team. While she fries up some animal flesh, I prepare the tub. She feeds. I baptize until a minor skirmish ensues over tub space. Isn't that always the way? I remove the loudest culprits from the foe and shepherd sopping wet, howling twins down the hall to their room, but they refuse to put on their Sophia undies and unicorn pajamas. What can I do?

I remember the wisdom of Angeles Arrien: "When we have stopped dancing, singing, being enchanted by stories, or finding comfort in silence is where we have experienced the loss of soul." So I perform a rather enchanting rendition of the Hokey Pokey in front of the closet mirrors, and although my gig needs work, it garners some attention.

"You put your right arm in, you put your right arm out, you put your right arm in, and you shake it all about, you do the hokey pokey, and you turn yourself around, that's what it's all about." Clap, clap.

After three rounds of Hokey Pokey with naked two-year-olds, Grammie is dizzy. I fall into the rocker, silent, and open my arms. They climb into my lap, two soft pink, satiated, warm bodies to embrace.

I feel the pace of the day begin to dissolve. Heart rates calm. The silence acts as a soothing balm. My eyes feel heavy. Was it really decades ago when I was rocking my own babies to sleep? I feel their hearts beating as they rest against me. Their worries fade, and the gentle rocking soothes the echoes of lonely sobs. I carry all of this inside of me, the burdens of my beloved, which over time become my pearl of great price.

As my hair continues to grey, I continue to search for the deeper meaning of life, but possibly, it's not in the thoughts and emotions that nettle our sensitive natures. Maybe it's when we allow a moment of silence to transform our emotions, living poetry, if you will, inviting the prose to gently engulf us as we enter the blessed rhythm of life.

10 MISCONCEPTIONS ABOUT MIDDLE-AGE

"The really frightening thing about middle age is that you know you'll grow out of it."
–Doris Day

Middle age is not a problem to be solved. It is a lifestyle to embrace and enjoy. Stop browsing long-term care insurance on the weekends. That's simply morbid and possibly detrimental to your health. It's our time to ride into the proverbial sunset without a map because it's all about the journey, not the destination. I love this quote by Hunter S. Thompson:

"Life should not be a journey to the grave with the intention of arriving safely in a pretty and well-preserved body, but rather to skid in broadside in a cloud of smoke, thoroughly used up, totally worn out, and loudly proclaiming, "Wow! What a Ride!"

I am no longer concerned about public opinion (that is only partly true, but it's so bold to claim). I want to enjoy the time I have left. My new directive is to worry less, laugh often, get out there and live. Brené Brown would say, "Strong back, soft front, wild heart."

"What does that mean?"

"I'm so glad you asked."

Let's start with our five God-given senses. It's time to ditch the carrot sticks (that was so 40s). Dine on foods you adore. Cram a cupcake in your lucious mouth. Fire up those amazing candles you've been hoarding for the last five decades. Touch each other. Hold hands. Kiss on the front porch. Give the neighbors something to talk about. Listen to music that feeds your soul, even if it's country. Get rid of anything hanging around the house that's an eyesore, including ugly bedding, clutter, and those half-dead poinsettias from Christmas. Read until three in the morning. Sleep in. Have DoorDash bring you a breakfast burrito. Do not explain yourself to others. Smile. Wave the naysayers away. There's a sixth sense, which we tend to ignore, called intuition. This improves with age. Trust it.

I realize some of us were raised with this silly notion that everyone should like us. That is preposterous and dangerous. Don't be blind to toxic individuals just because you assume everyone is working under the same premise. They aren't, and they'll destroy you. Create some distance. It's not your job to love everyone. That's why we have God and Raymond.

Brené Brown says, "I think midlife is when the universe gently places her hands upon your shoulders, pulls you close, and whispers in your ear: I'm not screwing around... Time is growing short." We have so much uncharted ground to explore in the second half of life. If we're trying to do this while carrying the weighty perceptions of others about who we are and what they think, we will not have the strength to reach the summit. This is your time, and as Brown says, "You're imperfect, and you're wired for struggle, but you are worthy of love and belonging." I say dig deep. Find the courage to live fully, to be seen, to show up for your own life because we're running out of time.

Common Misconceptions:
1. We're just sweet little old ladies (or men, I'm all about equality). Time to kick this one to the curb. *The truth is, I don't care what you think of me.* That's right. It's my new go-to statement. I'm thinking of having it tattooed across my palm for obvious reasons. It's not for everyone. No pressure.
2. Unseemly hair growth is a thing. It's not that hair growth is out of control, but it shifts as you age up. Breathe. I have a solution. The Girl Scout motto "be prepared" is our new gospel. So here's the deal—invest in good tweezers and magnifying mirrors (buy in bulk). You can never have too many. A rebel eyebrow can unexpectedly drop to the chin. Don't panic. Pluck it out and move on to the unattractive nose, ear, and toe hair. It's there. You just can't see it.
   I think a few warnings about hair removal ointments are in order here. They act on all types of hair! If you scratch your head, rub your eyes, or use the restroom while working with said products, the result is only humorous to your spouse, kids, relatives, friends, neighbors, and co-workers. The grandkids will also love it.
3. A flat tummy is essential. Get real. Tummies are highly overrated, and planking is clearly unethical. It's only a rumor, but I've heard high-waisted pants are making a comeback. "Woot, Hoot." They'll be in style for at least a decade. You might have some stored in the back of your closet from the '80s, and this, my friend, is where you put the tummy. If the rumors turn out to be false, refer to number one.
4. Wrinkles are the enemy. On Camazotz, from *A Wrinkle in Time*, all objects and places appear exactly alike because the entire planet must conform to the terrifying rhythmic pulsation of IT, a giant disembodied brain. I love Madeleine L'Engle and her quirky view of life. In her story, a wrinkle becomes the key element for passage to unknown dimensions. No truer statement has even been spoken. Let's not allow "It" to dictate our experience. Conformity is boring. Wrinkles are so in (along with

gray hair), but don't flaunt them because it makes the millennials jealous. Hide and seek is for kids. In Hinduism, upon the birth of your first grandchild, you become a "Forest Dweller." This is code for "It's time to celebrate you." Leaving the chores of managing a household behind, you are free to explore the bigger questions in life. Who the hell am I? Why am I here? Where am I going? Don't freak out. You do not have to be "born again" or sit under a Banyan tree in a grungy housecoat all day (I will not judge you if that is your choice).

5. This is your time to explore the aspects of life that resonate deeply within you. Time to Eat, Pray, Love, so to speak, like Elizabeth Gilbert. Your search for truth might include hummingbirds, tandem bikes, or discovering the best Pinot Noir in the South of France. You simply give yourself permission to become a seeker, move into spheres normally dominated by the heart, and go in search of you.

6. I'm not sizzling my way to 60. Have you given mentoring a thought? Stop whining. For those of you with decades of experience, it's time to pay it forward. Take someone under your wing. Share the wealth. It benefits both parties. Your base of knowledge does not matter. Someone is interested in parenting, selling, fashion, decorating, programming, investing, downsizing, creating, writing, educating, hiking, cooking, baking, gardening, traveling, praying, grieving, healing, meditating, acting, reading, or just being. Share, mentor, and connect because it's considered a sin to "leave your light under a basket." Put it on the nightstand, where it sheds light on others.

7. I've been moved to the Goodwill pile, unneeded and out of style. If you are lucky enough to have grandchildren, you are lucky enough. Enjoy them to the fullest. It is not possible for grandparents to spoil their grandkids. That is an urban legend. In study after study, they are finding a strong relationship between grandparents and grandchildren benefits both parties. Everyone longs for validation, acceptance, unconditional love, and, by the way, it's good karma (especially if you don't want to be a bug in your next life). Get on with the loving.

8. A word about naps: the answer is yes. If need be, refer to number one. Other than that, rest assured.

9. You can kiss your sex life goodbye. When it comes to sex, the general rule is quality over quantity, but this is not true for everyone. The only study I read on aging and sex claims middle-aged, monogamous women are enjoying it the most. I'm just putting this out there for future reference. Take advantage of the empty nest. It's not all about Netflix and running the dishwasher during non-peak hours. Something to keep in mind: please don't tweet about it at three in the morning. According to the children, this topic is still taboo. Let's keep it that way.
10. CRS (can't remember shit) is an actual condition. Not true. Be ready for an upgrade in your operating system. It's true. We process "differently" as we age, but recent studies claim we become smarter. Our brains continue to grow, along with our ears and nose, but that's irrelevant. We have better control of our emotions (which compensates for the bladder). We can focus on the positives because we have access to excellent wine. Problem-solving is easier (since most of your problems have moved out). People skills are stronger, along with the ability to see the big picture. That's right, millennials! We are one badass, determined, gritty group who can manage new situations with ease. The Boomers have arrived.
11. You have to be under 35 to enter a LuLuLemon store. Don't be a rule follower! Every study, blog, or essay on aging (including Oprah's) says to keep moving. The good news is our brains do not have to become strainers for pasta. We can keep them healthy by exercising, and this has subsequent benefits, like a healthy digestive system, sculpted muscles, and agility (both physical and mental). It's time to slip into some lycra and get moving. As part of our due diligence, Larry and I are walking to El Guapo's this afternoon for frozen margaritas and nachos. We're calling it research.

I don't have the "golden" answers to aging well, but I figure if I can't solve all the problems in the world, maybe I can refrain from adding to them. Doesn't that sound nice?

THE MEANING OF LIFE

"Hevel, hevel, everything is utterly hevel."
–Ecclesiastes 1:2

The search is on. What is the meaning of life, not just mine, but all life?

I'm obsessed with the word hevel. According to Jon Collins and Tim Mackie of the Bible Project, it appears thirty-eight times in Ecclesiastes, part of the wisdom literature, and loosely translates to smoke, vapor, or fog. Life can be shrouded, like fog, in mystery. It takes on many shapes, but try to grab it, and it slips right through your fingers. Life is complicated, confusing, disorienting, and unpredictable because when you're in a "fog," it's impossible to see the landscape clearly.

With the unexpected death of Kobe Bryant, I think everyone can agree on the unpredictable nature of life and the difficulty when maneuvering in the fog.

Hevel is a metaphor for life because, other than God, no one can understand the full scope and sequence of the lush mystery of our existence.

Is there relevance to life?

According to Ecclesiastes, the answer might not be what you want to hear.

What if life is meaningless?

Think about this, generations come and go, but the earth remains forever. The sun rises and sets. The wind blows. The oceans ebb and flow. People die. This is our common denominator, the great equalizer. Death devours the rich and the poor, the famous and the obscure, the good and the bad, the educated and the ignorant equally, and out of sequence, I might add.

Investing time, money, and emotion in the meaningless systems we have created is ridiculous, yet this is what we are trained to do. We live in a culture designed by Ford. We assemble people, conveying them through an educational system designed to mold them into workers. We teach strict adherence to rules and regulations, demote creativity, incite fear of the future, and above all, promote savings because the government is not going to take care of you. They're busy assembling the next generation of workers.

By the time one saves enough money to retire and go on that long dreamed of vacation, you're either too old to enjoy it, or there are unexpected travel restrictions. "It's all wretch and no vomit," as Alan Watts claims. You never get there.

I have seen something else under the sun: The race is not to the swift or the battle to the strong, nor does food come to the wise or wealth to the brilliant or favor to the learned; but time and chance happen to them all. Ecclesiastes 9:11

Good people die young. Bad people live long and profitable lives. There is no rhyme or reason to the randomness of life. It's as if we're all living in a pinball machine with God as wizard. The randomness of the cascading ball is clear. The flippers only add to the hevel because, eventually, we all end up in the queue.

The march of time does not stop. A hundred years from now, no one will remember you. You are a blip. The entire human race is a blip on the screen of life. In fact, our sun is only a tiny spark in time. As Don Miguel Ruiz claims, "Death is not the biggest fear we have; our biggest fear is taking the risk to be alive—the risk to be alive and express who we really are."

May I be so bold as to suggest a solution?

We need to turn things upside down.

We might be insignificant, and yet we're here. And as far as I know, this is the only planet in the galaxy that has an atmosphere that can support life. That's a miracle, and from this, we have been created.

Time, death, and the randomness of life might be the source of hevel. Life remains out of our control, and from our vantage, we lack clarity, but as Rachel Naomi Remen notes, "The willingness to consider possibility requires a tolerance of uncertainty."

If life is temporary or fleeting, what do we do with our days that give meaning to our lives, some purpose to our existence?

What is important are the things we can control. Read that again.

According to Ecclesiastes, we must accept the hevel, stop worrying about all the shit we can't control, and have faith that life does have meaning, even though we can't appreciate, or understand, the larger picture. As Jiddu Krishnamurti claims, "If you begin to understand what you are without trying to change it, then what you are undergoes a transformation."

What if we accept the life with which we are confronted and start moving from a position of not only tolerance but hospitality? Yes, we need money to survive, but what if we shifted our focus to that which is most important?

Family, friendships, a beautiful day, a loyal dog, a good book, a recess, if you will, from the daily grind?

Good Lord, let there be a conclusion.

Since we can't control life, stop holding on to it so tightly. Like Queen Elsa sings, "Let it go." We can work hard but also enjoy our lives, prioritize our loved ones. Set a nice table, sit down to a good meal, say grace, eat slowly, open a simple bottle of wine, taste our food, leave some scraps under the table for the dog, put down the phones, listen to each other, observe the beauty that surrounds you and those rare moments when you recognize the sacredness of all life.

Life might defy our comprehension, but it has meaning. We need to give ourselves permission to enjoy it and, in doing so, honor the sacredness of our existence and the God who created us. As Thomas Merton notes, "your life is shaped by the end you live for. You are made in the image of what you desire." You are a living miracle… remember this. Tattoo it on your heart. You survived your childhood. The bell has rung. Go out and play.

> *"Hevel, hevel, everything is utterly hevel."*
> **–Ecclesiastes 1:2**

MIDDLE-AGED PENANCE

"You know you've reached middle age when all you exercise is caution."
–Abraham Lincoln

I started boot camp a few days ago.

Let me just repeat, I STARTED BOOT CAMP A FEW DAYS AGO, and I can't move a single joint without massive, unbearable waves of pain shooting through my ravaged, anguished, depleted body, leaving me in the uncompromising predicament of not being able to assuage my overwhelming hunger, because a trip to the refrigerator is out of the question.

A few condolence cards in the mail, sympathizing with my deceased delectation, would be nice. I'm not exaggerating. I can barely type, let alone think, and did I mention I'm hungry?

At 11:30 last night, I had to get up and hobble to the kitchen for some pistachios. It's cold, and I'm only wearing underwear, so I bring the bowl of nuts back to bed. I snuggle under the blankets like a fat squirrel with her winter stash.

I'm peacefully eating my nuts when Larry says (he really yelled), "What the hell? Are you eating nuts in the middle of the night?"

Me, "crunch, crunch, crunch." It's my policy not to communicate with unreasonable people.

Larry, "Could you eat somewhere else? I'm trying to sleep. Jesus."

So he's kicking me out of bed in the middle of the night because I'm eating nuts? I couldn't stifle the giggle. It just slipped out.

Larry, "Some of us have to work tomorrow."

So I gather up my nuts and take them to the living room, where I decide I will stay all night as punishment for his rudeness. Then it occurs to me: why does he get the warm bed all to himself, and I'm on the couch?

Let me repeat, I STARTED BOOT CAMP A FEW DAYS AGO.

I finish my nuts and hobble back to my room. I have to turn on all the lights so I can brush my teeth. It's unfortunate that the drawer slams twice, and I did flush the toilet just to be annoying. (I know there's a water shortage, so I won't flush all day today.) He groans. I smile, married almost 39 years, and it's like the honeymoon never ends.

This morning, the minute I awake and reach for my iPhone, an electrical current of pain shoots through me like a bullet. Then I remember, I STARTED BOOT CAMP A FEW DAYS AGO.

With enormous courage, I push through the pain and check my blog hits. I'm obsessed and if you want to give me a total thrill, read my blog twice. Larry comes in with my coffee, the least he could do after the shenanigans last night. I give him my Meryl Streep look and remark, "Thank you, that's all."

He says, "Were you really eating nuts in the middle of the night?"

My policy is not to communicate with unreasonable people, so I just peer at him over the rim of my coffee cup. Then he says, "You were so quiet when you came back to bed," and I spit coffee all over the place.

I was bullied into returning to a second class this morning. Our dear friend Steve promises to join me, so all I can do is struggle into my big girl yoga pants and hobble to the car. I have acquiesced to a second round of penance for being middle-aged.

Joining the group at the Sports Park, I see Steve has already arrived, along with the peppy instructor. I'm exhausted after the warm-up. Our instructor talks us through the sets, keeping an upbeat voice and smiling like this is normal behavior for adults.

I somehow manage to get to the last part of the first set, which is step-ups. There is this two-foot cement block we're supposed to use as a prop, but I have to use both hands just to lift my leg onto the block.

I look at Steve, "There is no way I can do this?" I'm confounded by the others who are doing two sets of ten while chatting it up.

Steve says, "Use the bench over there. It's lower." He points to a small bench a few feet away.

I hobble over and sit down. Perfect. That's when the peppy instructor prods me to keep going. She is still smiling. I drag my sorry ass off the bench and succeed in one step up. She says, "Good job. You just needed a little confidence." What I need is a surrogate.

On my way home, I pull into Lunardi's parking lot to pick up a snack. I reckon I earned a treat, and now I have an entire grocery store. I am giddy with anticipation.

The phone rings. It's Steve, he says, "I just wanted to say you did a great job today."

I laugh, and say, "I can hardly walk. I sweat half my body weight, and now I'm at Lunardi's in search of a snack."

"Get the deli tuna. It's the best, and they'll let you sample."

I was going for the sushi, but I could try the tuna too? At first I grabbed a basket and then switch to a cart. I STARTED BOOT CAMP A FEW DAYS AGO, and I'm hungry.

The sourdough bread from Watsonville gets lobbed into my cart. I select two boxes of fresh sushi as an appetizer and head to the deli counter. After trying the tuna, the pasta salad, the potato salad, and then the macaroni salad, I'm not sure, but I think the server is annoyed with me.

She hands me a half pint of the tuna and then I have her throw in a ham quiche. On the way to the cashier, I grab two extra-large bags of sunflower seeds and a tub of cookies. I can't wait to get home: time to blog, eat and enjoy a pot of coffee all by myself.

When I pull into the garage, I realize Larry is still home. Shit. Should I leave all this food in the car? He'll think I'm insane.

Before I can figure out what to do, he opens the passenger door and grabs the bags of groceries off the seat. As he's unpacking, he doesn't say a word until he comes to the bags of nuts. Then he says, "You're not planning on eating nuts again tonight?"

But as you know, it's my policy not to communicate with unreasonable people, so I just smile.

IT'S A JUNGLE OUT THERE

"...it's amazing what passing the half-century mark does to free one to be eccentric."
–Madeleine L'Engle

Life is always under construction, but currently, so is my house. It feels as if I'm perpetually bewildered, unbalanced, and on the brink of the unknown. It's awkward, as if racing into the women's bathroom and realizing you are surrounded by urinals.

We celebrated Mother's Day in our backyard this year. Nic cooked his fabulous meatball lasagna. Kelley surprised us with appetizers from Sushi Confidential. Dante replenished the beer supply. Jim and Sue made a delicious dessert, but all I remember is the homemade whipped cream. Nancy arrived with gifts and fine wine. It was a full table with granddaughters and Shaggy milling about.

We were discussing, okay, disparaging, the design and functionality of my old kitchen. The one that has been gutted and carved as if a pumpkin at Halloween, and yes, I take everything personally because, as Kelley claims, "It's all about me."

Julie says, "When we were living here (note the appreciative tone), we needed two coffee pots because Dad's coffee tastes like muddy water."

Nic says, "Honestly, it wasn't drinkable."

Larry says, "It was plentiful and free."

Dante says, "They had three coffee pots cluttering the counter. There was no room to make toast."

Cheryl says, "Yeah, we had a pot for the muddy coffee, one for the millennials, and a Keurig for those of us who need a caffeine hit in the afternoon. But our circuitry is ancient. You can't have two things operating at the same time, or we blow a fuse."

Sue says, "Wait, why didn't I know about this?"

Larry says, "It's true. You can't run the toaster or microwave if the coffee is brewing, or everything blows."

Everyone looks at Larry as if he's missing a chromosome.

Sue says, "How long has this been going on?"

Cheryl says, "Thirty years."

Jim says, "Why am I not surprised?"

Julie says, "Nic and I would wait for Dad's coffeemaker to beep, and we'd run in from our room to hit the start button on our pot before Dad stuck his oatmeal in the microwave."

Cheryl says, "It was the Amazing Race, people sabotaging each other for energy usage. I was brutally condemned if I ran the dishwasher during prime time."

Nancy says, "I imagine, if the television were on the same circuitry, it would have been fixed decades ago?" (she is my sage)

She gets the look from Larry, who says with the practiced calm of a felon, says, "The entire house has been rewired. We can now run all the appliances in the kitchen even when the television is in use."

Julie says, "Perfect timing, Dad."

I had the perfect comeback, but I held my tongue because "I thought such awful thoughts that I cannot even say them out loud because they would make Jesus want to drink gin straight out of the cat dish," as Anne Lamott so beautifully states.

You're welcome.

Here's the actual issue I'm struggling to express but keeps eluding me.

How do you retire when you still have some fight left in you? It's as if I'm a caged tiger. After performing on demand for decades. I've been sold off to a local zoo.

By the first of June, I will have sixty summative projects to grade, final classes to conclude, co-workers to bid farewell to, and a LinkedIn account to retire.

I mean, who am I without a job? A retiree who spends her days watching reruns of the Magnum, P.I.?

The truth is most of us stay in occupations, homes, and even relationships long after they no longer serve us. In fact, they can be toxic, and yet we remain loyal, trustworthy, and professional until the bitter end. Why is that? If I were honest, I would say I fear living without purpose, of not being valued, of giving up the leverage a paycheck affords me, and of the security of being in close relationships, even imperfect ones.

Can I just admit I'm freaking out?! How will I spend my days? I won't have anyone to lecture, lesson plans to fuss over, papers to grade. My bank account and brain function will be as stagnant as a pond in the middle of summer. I'll have nothing to write about. WHAT WAS I THINKING?

Something could be wrong with me. I'll not only need to grieve these endings, but possibly organize a funeral. I've convinced myself that this is quite normal, and I'm pretty tight with my self-deceptive side, so please don't get between me and my delusions. It won't end well for you. Ask Larry.

When my mind is in the middle of massive gentrification, I try not to go in alone. That's why I write, so I don't have to chase my thoughts around as if a tiger chasing her tail. There is a children's story about this, but it's no longer considered politically correct (consider this your tiger trigger warning) and has been condemned by cancel culture, but strangely enough, I still find it a potent tale.

The story goes like this: a stylish kid goes for a walk when he encounters four covetous tigers and is forced to surrender his colorful new clothes, shoes, and umbrella so that they will not eat him. The tigers (symbolic of the way my thoughts behave) are vain, and each believes that they are better dressed than the others. The tigers have this massive argument and chase each other around a tree until they are reduced to a pool of butter. The kid then recovers his clothes and goes home. His father later collects the butter, which his mother uses to make pancakes.

This imagery is so deeply embedded in my subconscious that it surfaces when I'm trying to manage my internal conflicts. Outside the doors of my home, it's uncivilized. Envy is corrosive. Some things are not worth fighting over, but we can find resolution in a good meal with lots of butter. I've organized my life around this philosophy. How could it be canceled?

As John Vaillant notes, this is where the tension lies: tigers and people are actually very much alike. We are drawn to many of the same things, if for slightly different reasons. Both of us demand large territories. Both of us have prodigious appetites for meat. Both of us require control over our living space and are prepared to defend it, and both of us have an enormous sense of entitlement to the surrounding resources. If a tiger can poach on another's territory, it probably will, and so, of course, will we. A key difference, however, is that tigers only take what they need.

Really? And they've highjacked MY most fashionable vices?

As my tension reaches a crescendo, I think a new kitchen is not enough. I need a whole new house, a new religion, a new career, a new wardrobe, and maybe a therapist when what I really need is a long walk, a glass of water, and a medicinal movie with heavily buttered popcorn.

We don't need to be pleasant all the time or appeasing. We're enough with or without our crazy, circuit-blowing, disordered predicaments.

Silenced, placating, controlled people don't change the world. It's the uncaged, wild, living on the edge types who can abandon the trappings of modern culture with the bravery and majesty of a tiger.

We all need to decide if we're going to buy into this illusion of control or if we're going to honor the muddy, unappealing, flagrantly futile truth about being human: we're fragile, and it's a jungle out there.

GROW DAMN IT!

"Do you know what it means to come home at night to a woman who'll give you a little love, a little affection, a little tenderness? It means you're in the wrong house, that's what it means."
–Henny Youngman

You've heard the adage bloom where you are planted? Well, that sort of rubs me the wrong way. I start thinking about what kind of growth one should expect in the time of corona, with COVID for soil. And no fertilizer! My dad had a prominent sign he used to stake in his garden. It said, "Grow

Damn It," which sums up his aptitude for nurturing to perfection. Now I'm thinking that might be my new motto.

Or the name of my first book?

After spending the majority of my imposed quarantine commingling with my spouse, I'm rethinking the rash decision to coalesce my parent's ashes in a posh urn up at the lake. Glancing up at the bell-shaped ceramic vase, I scan for signs of discontent, but all appears placid and calm as the lake. Anna Quindlen says, "The single most important decision you will have to make is not where to live, or what to do for a living, it's who you will marry," and maybe remind your kids it's not until we tire of each other, it's unto death do you part.

I jest. Slightly.

The indisputable truth remains, my parents thoroughly enjoyed each other's company (I'm sure it thrills them to be eternally potted together). They could not have realized it at the time, but living in the shadow of their love story was the best gift they could have given Nancy and me. They built a worthy foundation, and even though I'm as ancient as hell, it continues to inform my life.

I admit I do not run to dab perfume behind my ear and pinken my lips before Larry walks in the door as mom did for dad, but I smile if we're not in a fight.

I'm sure he's just as charmed.

Don't think I'm so naïve as to think my parents' marriage was perfect. It was not, and, like everyone else, day after day, they had to decide if they would coax the good out of each other or the bad. Some days, I think the entire deal pivoted on my dad's sense of humor and a decent amount of wine.

If this seems abstract, let me solidify my point. Every relationship I've ever had, I hold up to that of my parents, not intentionally. It's what I know. Larry not only made the cut, but he overachieved, and I'll tell you why. He's steadfast, hardworking, and not prone to gossiping. In fact, he rarely speaks, but that's beside the point. He's the one I dare to dream with, laugh until I pee my pants, and even though we fight so fiercely, I start googling lawyers on my iPhone, maybe that's where we *Grow Damn it,* in the long crawl back to each other. He's a good man. The kind of man my dad always hoped I would find. This, for me, is the essence of a quality individual, because everyone has the capacity to be wicked. It's the ones who choose not to who interest me, and he makes great… coffee.

Thinking back on my family of origin helps me identify the origins of some of my most deeply held beliefs.

Family dinner was a standard practice when I was growing up. The four of us ate together almost every night. It was expected and protected, no phone calls, no leaving the table before being excused, and no food left on your plate (even if it was liver). Occasionally, my dad used the dining table as a podium, and his message was always the same, "If you grow up to be half as smart as your mother, you'll be fine. She's the smartest person I know and the best mother." I remember thinking, poor daddy, he'll never be as smart as mom, and we all depend on him.

Dad was a generous provider, but the message he left with us was even more profound. His devotion to my mother was a physical reflex he had absolutely no control over. I loved that about my dad.

My parents started their life together in the shadow of the Korean war, the Great Depression, and the end of the Golden Age. A new era of liberalism would replace that of compliance and conformity. Maybe that's why I'm so confused.

Walking down the long aisle of Mission Santa Clara on our wedding day, flanked by both my parents, I could not have imagined the length and breadth of our journey together, those passages I prefer to forget right next to the unforgettable ones. There were visits to the emergency room for ear infections, stitches, and broken bones, but also skidding into the parking lot, water dripping down my legs, and coming home with a new life.

We had absolutely no clue, but we did it anyway, and when the storms came, we knew they would eventually run out of rain. Losing jobs, reinventing ourselves, holding the keys to a lake house, all doors in the long corridor of life that we dared to open. As my brother-in-law, David Wood, was known to say, "It's all good."

We still have riveting discussions about politics, novel career paths, risky investments, and dinner options, but today, most of our conversations go like this:

Are we going to the lake?

I don't know.

We talked about it yesterday.

I wasn't listening.

You never listen.

You always say that.

What did we decide?

I can't remember.

My daughter Kelley and her fiancé, Tim had to make the heartbreaking decision to reschedule their wedding during this pandemic. We are all feeling their despair, and I look forward to the day I can watch her make the long walk down the aisle of marriage. It's strange how we cleave to our old ways of being in the world before the virus, the quarantine, the mayhem of putting our lives on hold. Maybe this is how we hold it together when imprisoned by the harsh tactics of a virus, one that terrorizes us with fear, "Stay put. Stay inside. Stay away from each other." Yet I'm plagued (couldn't resist) by the memories of what was once my reality.

The labor of letting go reminds me of childbirth. I remember having to surrender to the contractions, the pain, and the pressure of something I created, but was ready to survive on its own. The only thing left for me to do was to push, push a part of myself out into a chaotic world. If you know me at all, you know I resist severing cords because separation from a beloved way of being means confronting the unknown, and that's not good for Cheryl.

All I can say is thank God I found the "one special person I want to annoy for the rest of my life," says Rita Rudner. And while I'm still certifiably sane, if they pot Larry and me together for all eternity, I want a swanky urn from Bloomingdales! If you're trying to bloom in the middle of this blasted pandemic but need a sign, feel free to use my dad's, *Grow Damn It.*

PART III: MONUMENTAL

WHEN YOU HIT ROCK BOTTOM

"We rise by lifting others."
–Robert Ingersoll

It's pouring down rain in the middle of the day. Both Mom and I are bottom down, reeling in defeat, on the wet pavement not twenty feet from the car. The day didn't start out this way. There were no warning signs or ominous premonitions, but you know how God likes to shake things up, especially when we've become complacent or confounded.

Napoleon Hill claims, "Every adversity, every failure, every heartache carries with it the seed of an equal or greater benefit." Not what I was thinking at the time. More pressing issues had my focus, but after a laborious reflection came clarity and insight.

The day begins at 5:50 a.m. when my floral-covered cell phone starts beeping. It takes three seconds to figure out how to turn off the horrid sound. I take a deep breath and give a brief nod to God as I review the logistics of the day. If I get up right now, Mom and I will have enough time to enjoy a cup of coffee before dressing and arriving at the Stanford Treatment Center by 7:15 a.m. We are professionals at this whole infusion thing. This is our fourth round of chemo, and believe me when I say, "We have it down."

I've become the unsung doorman (woman) as I maneuver no less than three bags, two lukewarm coffees, one set of keys, and an unstable mother from condo to car. Juggling these obstacles like a seasoned clown, I feel the need to Snapchat, but that's not part of my skill set, and I might drop something. So my talents remain undocumented as I move our little entourage towards the carport. There is a moment when I stand back, watching her laborious movements, and I can't help but acknowledge how her courage strengthens my own.

When mom, bags, and walker are safely stowed in the car, we hit the road—this is when I'm seized by a powerful urge to drive away from it all—the cancer, the treatments, empty pillboxes, labs, errands, chauffeur duties, sleep-deprived, appointment driven life, but that would be a mistake, because this is exactly where we need to be, in this space, and time. I happen to have a schedule that permits me the privilege of time. It's my currency, and I'm a big spender (Ask Larry). My third child Tony told me on the phone just last week, "It doesn't matter how hard it is. Stay present. You will look back someday and appreciate every moment." A wise young man indeed.

Rabbi Harold Kushner says if you can concentrate on finding what is good in every situation, you discover that your life will suddenly be filled with gratitude, a feeling that nurtures the soul.

We arrive at the center just as the sun is peeking through the clouds. It's a sign, right? These gigantic picture windows surround the entire facility. The scenery explodes in front of us with this glorious ray of light breaking through the pall. A storm cloud is forming off the horizon (which I choose to ignore). I focus instead on the lush green mountains that surround our valley, divided by a maze of intricate roadways teaming with toy cars. I am mesmerized. Clearly, God has a hand in this day, and I claim it as good. Mom is called in for labs. I get to sit in the waiting room with the bags, cold coffee, and the view. Winning.

This is when things get sticky. Her veins are difficult to find. Some have collapsed, and they've compromised the rest. This is not good for chemo. After two stabs in search of a good vein, the lab tech moves us to the treatment center to let the RN have a 'stab' at it (I can't resist). She finds a good one, bless her heart, and finally gets the much-anticipated sample of blood to the lab. It seems as if, as a woman, I'm always dealing with blood, waste products, and bodily functions. (Compost for a future book?)

The news is not good. Her white blood count is too low for treatment today. Disappointment is the ranking emotion. Like being cut from the team, we feel rejected. I want to cry, but I'm afraid I'll never be able to stop, so I remain stoic. After three and a half hours, they give her a shot of Nuprin and send us home with a follow-up appointment for next week. We drive back to the house in silence. I send Larry a text update with a sad emoji.

Xavier Le Pichon reminds me that by walking with the suffering person who has come into your life and whom you have not rejected, your heart progressively gets educated by them. They teach you a new way of being. Fabulous, now I know how it feels to be defeated.

This time, getting the bags, the walker, Mom, and two empty coffee cups back into the house seems as if we're retreating from an overwhelming battle. We land in our chairs in the living room and listen to the news. Glum is a good word for our current dispositions. I look at mom. I know she knows I know… it's our communion. I think this is what Jesus tried to teach us.

Larry sends a text, "Let's head up to the lake."

Me, "Bring mom?"

"Hell yes, if she's up for it." (I'm wondering if he is up for it?)

I present the idea to mom. She practically leaps out of her chair, not really, but she spews directions as if an army sergeant, "I'll need the nightie hanging on the bathroom door, fresh underwear, my pills, a toothbrush, my phone, the port-a-potty, a bottle of Gatorade, my cleanser, cream, Vaseline…" At least she doesn't have to deal with hair products. I spring into action, racing back and forth from car to house, loading our gear.

After helping mom into her muted red raincoat, I grab the sturdy walker, the one we use for ambitious outings, and we begin the slow march back to the car. On the way, I pause to thank God for the collapsed veins and low White blood cell counts. It's as if my original urge to drive away from it all has been divinely answered.

We are twenty feet from the car, maneuvering down a gentle slope onto the carport when her legs give out. Unexpectedly. She goes down. I lung for her, wrapping my arms around her small frame, slowing her descent to the ground. I tried, but I could not keep her from falling. Now I'm wondering if this divinely inspired outing might be a fool's errand after all.

I panic and attempt to yank her off the ground.

She remains perfectly calm. She says, "Let me rest a minute, Cheryl." Keep in mind it's pouring rain, and we are not sheltered.

I sit down beside her and say, "Mom, we have to get you back into the house."

She bristles at my words. "No, I'm going to the lake."

I'm aghast. "Mom, you're too weak."

She is not budging. "No, we're going."

I move on to more practical issues. "Mom, let's get you off the ground, and then we'll decide."

She's more determined than Malala Yousafzai, "I'm going."

I move behind her, place both my arms around her middle, and lock my hands together. "Okay, on the count of three." I lift. She pushes. Nothing. I can't lift 116 pounds of my beloved mother off the wet ground. What the hell? We try again, "mom, push with your legs." She tries but to no avail. I call on dad, "A little help here. Your bride is sitting on the wet pavement in the pouring rain." On the third try, I miraculously get her off the ground and onto the small seat on the walker. We look at each other, the rain dripping off our noses. I'm completely traumatized. Yes, I have the urge to Snapchat, but I resist. She points to the car.

As Kathleen Bamford says, "It is when we are confronted with… poignant reminders of our mortality that we become most aware of the strangeness and wonder of our brief life on Earth." This will be mom's final lesson that she will bequeath me. Life is precious. Don't waste a minute worrying about the things you can't control. Be brave. Do what you can with what you've been given.

The lake is not up for discussion. I settle her gently into the passenger seat, and we drive away from it all—the cancer, the treatments, empty pillboxes, errands, chauffeur duties, sleep-deprived, appointment-driven life, and we head to the lake. It's exactly what we need, at precisely the right moment. And Kate Braestrup says it beautifully, "... a miracle can only be the resurrection of love beside the unchanged fact of death."

THE ARROGANCE OF TIME

"How did it get so late so soon? It's night before it's afternoon. December is here before it's June. My goodness how the time has flewn. How did it get so late so soon?"
–Dr. Seuss

In my remote cocoon rolled up in a blanket secured to the double-wide chair I used to loathe and now love, gazing out over the expanse of the lake, the steadfast mountain, the "unmentionable" fog, I'm thinking about the arrogance of time and how swiftly we mutate, as if a caterpillar from chrysalis to adult.

I am often deceived by the endless charm of time, disguised as a gift, but somehow pompous as a politician whose false assurances serve no one.

You know what I mean?

The conceit of a system so dedicated to its own perpetuation it fails those it's obligated to assist, one who is incapable of turning back his scrawny arms of time, always marching forward, as if a well-trained soldier who refuses to stop the trajectory of the front line, oblivious to the multiplicities it has overrun, left in ruins, laid flat in its overarching objective to never surrender to the moment.

Fuck you is the epithet I want to use, but I'm silenced by my dowdy manners as I dig for the right words to describe what I nurture in my mind, this persistent unease, similar but not the same as grief, a sort of angst that has settled into my bones.

Time and death seem to be marching in formation, and I'm annoyed with their ruthless precision.

Speaking of marching... carrying box after box across the street, my daughter Julie, son Dante and son-in-law Nic, wrestle with a life's worth of valuables, stashed for a year in my garage and now being re-conveyed to a new dwelling... clothing, linens, toys, plates, spices, Tupperware, couches, cushions, and mirrors followed by tables, dressers, beds, and bikes. The movement back and forth across the street reminds me of a beehive as the workers gather their loot, returning to the hive with the queen bee (Julie) directing the entire production.

Julie says, "Honey, do we really need this?"

"Mom, is this couch too heavy for you to lift?"

"Dante, can you help us carry this into the house?"

"Dad, when you finish putting in the new toilet, can you start on the bunk beds for the twins?"

After two days, Larry and I escape to the lake to rest our weary muscles and recover our ailing limbs. Our exhaustion is as mysterious to us as our grey hair and wrinkles. How did we arrive at old age where energy is as extravagant as premium gasoline?

Larry says to me, "It feels good to be back up here after such a long break." He seems so relaxed, smiling as he opens a nice bottle of GiaDomella Cab, splashing a taste into each of our glasses. This wine is the divine vision of our dear friends Vicky and Rich Passalacqua, who establish GiaDomella Wines using the grapes from their family vineyards. Trust me, it's blessed, something Jesus would have approved, and served at Cana.

I nod my head but totally disagree. Not with the wine, with the way we view our time at the lake. We both live in want of being in the place we are not. We'll call it irreconcilable desires, a flume we'll never bridge. Being here and not being here is simply how I measure time.

"Come back" are words I rotate as if laundry in the drum of my mind. Seriously, I'm haunted by these spinning thoughts, and, as you know, if I need to deal with it, so do you.

I want to be at the lake (think writing, water, wineries). He longs for the established routines of our home in the Bay Area (think biking, breakfast, and boot camp). What keeps us apart is what we think we need. Isn't that always the case?

After I stacked the dishes in the washer, wiped the counters clean, with the smell of pan-fried ribeye's still lingering in the air, we retire to the long green couch. Sipping the last of the red wine, watching the glowing embers of a Duraflame log fade, discovering again the seduction of wordless moments, the endless ticking of the clock. Both of us lost in our own thoughts.

We sit, this man and I, our aging bodies so different from when we first met, closer now to the end than to the beginning of life, as he rubs life back into my icy feet, the dog, as if a needy child, wedged between us. The winter is barren, just like me. I gaze at the rippling moon river reflected on the placid lake envied by the stars, as I envy the spring from the perspective of winter.

I wonder about the world my granddaughters will inhabit, one that I will never know, or the world that has passed away, one that they will never understand. And I worry that this entire year spent sheltering in place, suspended, unheralded, trapped in the amber of the moment, is the year we collectively failed to seize.

Our home of thirty years will be dismantled when we return, as the kids vacant our guest rooms. We prepare to demolish the old tile in the kitchen and tear out the dysfunctional appliances, cabinets, and even some walls, essentially refurbishing the hearth of our home as inhumanly as fire extirpates a forest.

Kelley is coming home in a few days, maybe to see it all one last time before the demolition, perhaps to capture some unretrievable moment in time?

I've lived most of my life with unfashionable finishes. Part of me wants this new kitchen, so in some rare form of insanity, I, too, can be redone. As

Jennifer Elisabeth says, "Don't worry if people think you're crazy. You are crazy. You have that kind of intoxicating insanity that lets other people dream outside of the lines and become who they're destined to be."

Julie said to me in the car the other day, "Your past self doesn't need you, but your future self does." That sort of stopped me in my tracks. What am I doing today to enhance my destiny?

We have three days up at the lake before we return to the nest, the upheaval, the metamorphosis. Our trinity of days will be filled with trips to Lakeport in-between hours of work, walks in the neighborhood, quiet dinners for two, slumbering quietly beside each other as we have for decades.

We've taken to enjoying our coffee in bed under the cover of morning, him watching the news, me writing these words, lost in our own reveries. The process is slow, lumbering, and gentle. This is who we've become?

He works at the game table, which, as you know, is cattywampus to the long green couch, with me at the generous kitchen counter. I preemptly take down the "Save water. Drink wine." sign, so my students won't see this aspect of their teacher, pristine, neutered, sub rosa. We're studying the Holocaust this week, determining the depth of evil man is capable of enacting on those considered subhuman, without dignity, inferior. Is it not so different today? How we scapegoat others when we refuse to shoulder the burdens of our own decisions.

I can't help but wonder what might happen in the throes of a pandemic, with an invisible enemy, one who has defeated us in the most catastrophic of ways, one who targets the vulnerable and severs our ability to breathe, zapping our strength, diminishing our reason. A nemesis who has taken down our global economy and wreaked havoc on all our lives, although some are more heinous than others. Who will be left to blame?

Our time at the lake is fruitful. The days pass quickly. Our work here is done, but as Markus Zusak says, "She wanted none of those days to end, and it was always with disappointment that she watched the darkness stride forward."

As we carry our bags to the car, fastening the dog cover to the back seat, resting our coffees in the cupholder before driving away from all that I desire, I hear the words "Come back" echo in my mind, pushing away the needs, the wants, the obligations that are calling us home.

What I'll be missing tomorrow is you next to me on the long green couch, sipping wine by the flickering embers of a Duraflame log, discovering the seduction of wordless moments, moon rivers, and pitch-dark nights. Oh, the arrogance of time, "Come back." I'm not finished fanning the embers of an aging courtship. I just put a dab of perfume behind my ear.

THE MERRY GO ROUND

"Compassion brings us to a stop, and for a moment we rise above ourselves."
–Mason Cooley

The bed is warm, but it's not my own. I'm curled up in the fetal position, on high alert, waiting for her soft call in the dark. I go to her at midnight, at four in the morning, and again at seven. She's weak, disoriented, and dependent on my strength. This is a vocation of love, one I willingly accept, but I'm emerging from the rubble as a new creation.

The disparity between my inner and outer reality is alarming. I thought I knew myself better than this, but it turns out I was all wrong. Today, I'm feeling judgmental, impatient, and slightly unkind. Repeatedly. Observing myself from a safe distance, I keep a close eye on this warrior woman occupying my body. I can't figure out where she came from or how to get rid of her. She does not budge an inch for me or anyone else who gets in her way. You go, girl. This is not my usual demeanor, but I appreciate her efficacious nature, especially when she's putting a dent in the Blue Shield, trying to wrestle a security code from the guy with a Napoleon complex, or battling with customer service over network status.

"I need the security code to the front gate tonight. We have a caregiver coming tomorrow morning, and she needs access." In a calm voice, the warrior woman is explaining her situation for the fifth time to the ornery gatekeeper.

"I just answer the phones, miss."

"Is this not a twenty-four-hour emergency number for the front gate?"

"Everyone's gone for the holiday. I just answer the phones."

"There has to be someone I can call."

"That's my job. I called Mr. Napoleon after your last call, but he doesn't give out the code."

"Give me Mr. Napoleon's number."

"I can't do that, miss."

"We're going in circles here. Give me your name. Maybe the police can help." (I'm bluffing but determined.)

(He hangs up on me?)

A minute later, my sister's phone rings. It's Mr. Napoleon himself. (He thought Nancy would be more reasonable. He was wrong.)

"We need the security code tonight. We have help coming tomorrow morning and they need access."

"I won't give out the code."

"How are they supposed to get in?"

"You could meet them here."

"Are you kidding? We'll just make fifteen keys and give them out to everyone we know. I'm sure that's much better than giving one person the code. Thank you for your time. You've been absolutely worthless. Good night." (Booyah)

How does one deal with gatekeepers? Sometimes I think the world has gone mad. Round and round, we go with just about every service, appointment, and network we encounter. I refuse to give up.

"I'm sorry, miss. You're out of network. We cannot see your mom tomorrow."

"I was on the phone with Blue Shield for two hours. We made this appointment over two weeks ago. My mom is very sick, and you wait until the day before her appointment to cancel. This is unconscionable."

"Miss."

"Blue Shield, set up this appointment. This is ridiculous."

"Miss."

"How is a sick person supposed to see a doctor with such a screwed-up healthcare system? No one is taking new patients. Every plan has a major flaw, and the lexicon is indiscernible."

"Miss."

"What do you recommend I do?"

"You need to call this number and have them update your status."

I called, waiting for thirty minutes on hold. The customer service guy was nice, but uninformed. "I can't do anything from here. I think you need to talk to someone else."

"Who?"

"I don't know."

I call the doctor back in a rather sordid mood, "You gave me the wrong number. I had to wait thirty minutes to talk to someone who can't help me. My mother is coming to this appointment tomorrow. You will have to call Blue Shield and figure this out yourself."

"I'm not sure you are covered."

"We're covered and approved. I think they did not update the system because of the holiday weekend. And please don't call my mother and drag her into this. She's not feeling well, and you upset her for no reason. I am approved to make her medical appointments."

"I'll have to recheck your status."

"Look, I think we got off to a poor start and I'm appealing to you as one woman to another. I could care less about policies. I'm just trying to get my mother to a doctor. You are in the healthcare field, and we need help. My mother has two insurance policies. They assigned us to this doctor, and we can't wait another day."

"Okay, okay, come early. There's a mountain of paperwork to fill out."

"I'll bring my own pen. Thank you."

Even when the situation seems absurd, I believe in civility.

I remember when I was just a young girl, maybe four or five. My mom brought me to the local park. I sprinted from the car and jumped on the merry-go-round but the older kids didn't want me to join. I got one leg over the bar as the kids pushed the merry-go-round faster and faster. This left me hopping on one leg or get thrown to the ground and stomped on by an endless parade of legs. I panicked. Just when I thought I was losing my grip, the merry-go-round came to an abrupt halt. Turning around, I found my mama grasping the bars with both hands, dragging her body across the rough gravel, using all her strength to stop the momentum so I could get off safely. Her knees were bloody. I remember her dignified anger, and the way she stared down those mean girls. She was a warrior woman that day, and I was ever so proud. Okay, relieved, and proud.

In the midst of all this chaos, the most unexpected thing happens. It always does. Just when I've lost all hope in humanity, someone comes along and restores my denigrated soul. We struggle from the car to the doctor and back to the car. Mom is exhausted, and we still needed to get lab work done. I push ahead, dropping her off on a bench in the shade, racing off to park the car, and jogging back to the bench. The long walk to the office, the endless lines, the medical cards, the signatures, and the wait. I'm not sure she'll have enough energy to get back to the car.

The nurse who is signing us in can see the panic in my eyes, and she responds like a human, "Come on in here, honey. Bring your mom. We'll just get this sample right now." Her name is Linda. Mom plops into the chair, head leaning against the wall, eyes closed. I don't think she realizes this nurse took us in front of all these other people, but I do. She is ever so gentle. "A slight pinch, honey. I'm sorry. Here we go, almost done, sweetheart." I'm stunned. My eyes water. I blink and fight back the emotions threatening to overcome me. Linda finishes and gently places a Band-Aid on the wound. "All done." In a very soft voice, mom says, "Thank you." I help her stand, looking to the ground because the unsaid thank you is spilling from my eyes. Linda notices. She reaches for my arm and gives me a supportive squeeze. I cannot speak. I've been hopping on one foot for months when this complete stranger reaches out and stops the uncontrollable spin with undeserved kindness.

When evening has settled around me like a warm blanket, I watch this warrior woman resting up for the next battle. She's curled up in the fetal position, in an unfamiliar space, waiting for the labor to begin.

LIFE TURNS ON SMALL CHOICES

"Perhaps it's that you can't go back in time, but you can return to the scenes of a love, of a crime, of happiness, and of a fatal decision; the places are what remain, are what you can possess, are what is immortal. They become the tangible landscape of memory, the places that made you, and in some way you too become them. They are what you can possess and in the end what possesses you."
–Rebecca Solnit

I thought I would know, instinctively, innately, that an inkling would prickle the back of my neck and send shock waves down the length of my spine, but that didn't happen. I remained blissfully unaware until I was regrettably informed, dangling from the hands of a clock by my fingernails.

There were insignificant chores to be done, a prescription to pick up, a hostess gift to buy, and some last-minute food shopping to do before slipping into my car and heading home, gloriously normal for fifteen more minutes.

I've learned from people who enjoy delineating these things that there are 1440 minutes in a day, which makes me question how a single second can change everything, sending one's life on an igneous trajectory. As Ahmad Ardalan says, "Sometimes in life, a sudden situation, a moment in time, alters your whole life, forever changes the road ahead."

It took five minutes to put the groceries away before grabbing my computer from my room and heading out back to grade a few assignments in the comfort of the cool patio. Of course, I have to make a cup of coffee and adjust the curtain for shade before opening Google Classroom.

There are sixty-five papers to grade. I'll admit it's daunting, so I reach for my iPhone, purposely avoiding that which needs to be done.

This is when I notice a missed call from an unknown number. Curious?

After clicking the voicemail message, I listen to the principal of Notre Dame, who's calling me on her personal cell phone. The time is 1:15 p.m.

"Hi Cheryl, this is Mary Beth. I'm calling from my cell phone. We had an odd experience in the front office today. Someone called and said they were your son, Dante. He wanted your phone number and, as you know, we don't give out private information. He called from this number... but the name on the phone was Jaime. It seemed a little strange, and I wanted to let you know."

That seems strange, but I thought maybe Dante's phone died (not the first time). He's been working out-of-town all week, and he tried calling me from a co-worker's phone but didn't have my number memorized.

I dial the number.

A deep male voice says, "Hello."

"Hi, this is Cheryl Oreglia. I received a message..."

He abruptly interrupts, "Yes, this is Jamie. I'm a paramedic. Your son Dante has been in an accident. He's okay, but I took him to Kern Medical Trauma Center as a precaution for further testing."

It's the call no parent ever wants to receive because there are some memories you can never fully erase.

I could form one word, "Dante?"

The rest of the conversation is a complete blur, high-speed accident, rollover, fire, Good Samaritan, injuries incurred, car totaled.

With a single glance at my terrorized face, Julie and Nic spring into action. Tears streaming unchecked down my cheeks, knees shaking, I'm the epitome of calm in an emergency.

Nic pulls up the phone number and address of the Kern Trauma Center in Bakersfield on his computer. Julie alerts her dad, but all I can think about is getting to my son, alone in a hospital, four hours away.

Larry says, "Cheryl, pack a bag. We might have to stay overnight." I move numbly to my room, grab a tote, throw in pajamas, my computer, and wander back into the kitchen. Suddenly, nothing in my life makes any sense.

Julie says, "mom, think about what you need," but I can't comprehend a single word she is saying. I fail to pack just about everything I would need for an overnight, including underwear, deodorant, or a toothbrush!

Nic has Dante's nurse on the phone. She can give Dante a message, but we can't talk to him. I question nothing. "Tell him we're coming. We love him. We'll be there soon."

The next thing I know is we're barreling down the 101. The traffic is as dense as the silence is deafening. Keeping my emotions in check is impossible, so I just give up and let the tears flow.

I start making these little deals with God. "Okay, if I could just get to Bakersfield immediately, I'll refrain from cursing. I'll serve the poor. I'll stop complaining about what you've done to my skin."

Why does time pass so slowly when you need it to pass quickly? Neale Donald Walsch says, "… time is experienced as a movement, a flow, rather than a constant. It is you who are moving, not time." Or the damn traffic.

Not helpful.

Time should be equal as it passes through our lives, but it's not, and right now, I believe it's the root cause of an inordinate amount of angst.

The I5 is straight, scaly, as if a snake of concrete, merciless, endless, and deadly.

Like boulders in the road, these enormous trucks randomly pull into the fast lane and cause all sorts of unnecessary delays. Suddenly, I'm cussing like a truck driver again. "Sorry, God."

Larry remains unscathed, focused, and unavailable.

There's an endless number of exits, all leading onto artery roads. I notice how they dissolve into the barren landscape. The traffic is as thick as blood, and we've become an immeasurable pulse in time, hammering our way along a corroded vein to Bakersfield. My brain is despondent, it aches. I find myself clutching my arms around my middle and rocking in the seat.

I'm thinking back to the day Dante was born. He wouldn't come out of his womb (not much has changed). On my last visit, the doctor estimated his weight at approximately nine pounds, and now we were both motivated to expel this overdue child. My mom had arrived on a morning flight to manage the household while Larry and I drove to Good Samaritan Hospital, where I would be coaxed into labor with a new seaweed process. I'm nine months and one week into my fourth pregnancy. I no longer care if the method is natural and less stressful for the baby. Did I mention the nine pounds?

Larry stayed for several hours, walking the halls of the hospital with me, hoping to start some action in my womb. Nothing.

All night, every other hour, they applied a seaweed poultice to my cervix. By dawn, I was exhausted, tired of hearing other women screaming in the throes of labor, until finally feeling the initial tugs of mild contractions myself.

I called Larry from the bathtub because I heard that if it were false labor, it would stop if you were bathing, but the contractions were becoming stronger by the minute.

I said, "It's time."

He was at my door in ten minutes.

Mind you, I had been telling everyone all night, including the janitor, that I wanted an epidural. I had the first three children naturally, and I didn't want to feel a single contraction with my fourth. Keep in mind—nine pounds.

The nurses came and went, each time with me begging for the anesthesiologist to numb me from the spine down, but to no avail. Larry took matters into his own hands, and for once, I was overjoyed.

He went into the hall and started screaming, "Where is the fucking anesthesiologist? My wife needs one now!"

When he returned to the room, I said, "Honey, I need to push," and I struggled to get into position.

You've never seen a man scramble, multitask, and panic all at once until you tell him you're pushing, and he is the only one in the delivery room.

While he's pushing the emergency buttons on my bed, I'm pushing this baby out of the womb. His hands are in position, I'm in position, but he looks as if he's ready to catch a football instead of a nine-pound baby.

I hold my breath and bear down.

He moans.

Finally, the nurse arrives. She says, "Yes, she's at ten. Let's get this boy out."

The room fills with doctors and nurses. Dante is showing distress. He needs to come out with the next contraction, come hell or high water. The nurse ends up laying on my stomach to assist with my exhaustive and unproductive pushing.

Larry looks faint.

The doctor says, "There he is. Okay, stop pushing. He's got a cord wrapped around his neck."

Only a mother could stop pushing in the middle of a contraction because she knows her child's life depends on it. I breathe, squeeze Larry's hand as if a vice, and, with all my strength, remain idle through the rest of the contraction.

Crisis resolved. The cord is untangled, and Dante, all 9 pounds, 4 ounces of him, takes his first breath as the nurse places him in my arms. His eyes are wide open, and it's as if he were gazing into my soul.

Watching the tumbleweeds blowing along the highway, I notice my breathing is labored. I'm holding tight to Larry's hand and feel as if I'm sitting idle in the middle of life's most horrific event. As my heart painfully contracts, I'm holding on with all my strength until he is in my arms.

I'm as lost as the disciples in a storm, complete with Jesus, lounging in the backseat, scolding me about my capricious faith.

The hours tick by at a snail's pace. God ignores my gratuitous offers until we pull off the freeway, and suddenly I feel as if my prayers have been answered. Dante Alighieri says, "Oh how time hangs and drags till our aid comes," and I'm thinking my son must be feeling much the same.

We have the nurse on the phone, and she informs us, "Only one person can go in," and that will be me. It's not up for negotiation.

I slap on my mask and run towards the flashing emergency sign, passing through the automatic doors, that part as if the Red Sea, and into an abandoned waiting room. Yellow crime tape blocks the empty chairs from use.

A nurse leans out of her cubicle. She says, "Can I help you?"

"My son Dante Oreglia was admitted earlier today after a car accident, and I'm here to pick him up." Suddenly, I feel as if I can't breathe.

"Wait outside, please," and the Red Sea comes crashing down, an insurmountable barrier between me and my son. What I want to do is storm the doors and blitzkrieg every room until I find him, but I swallow this impulse, as if bile, and quickly exit the building.

How often do we find ourselves on the outside looking in? I'm pacing with a community of rough-looking characters, all waiting for someone, each of us lost in our own misery. We recognize in each other that which we hold in common, overwhelming despair, and I feel my compassion swell.

Some guy is crouched over, holding his belly. His hair is unkempt, and he appears to be coming off some sort of drug addiction. His sweatpants are soiled, and he stands, moaning in agony, not five feet from me. I silently do the same. Another man in baggy jeans and a plaid shirt is smoking a cigarette as he leans against the banister. He, too, is mimicking my worry. Two women wearing tattered jeans and tank tops sit together on the cement steps looking at their phones, but I notice their arms touching and the worry they carry in their tiny frames.

I wait. I fret. I sniffle and silently moan.

After what seemed an eternity but most likely was only minutes, Dante walks through the automatic doors. The body I lovingly made is whole, disheveled, and in my arms. I'll admit to a complete loss of composure. It happens. The relief wracking my body comes in the form of sobs. This is when I notice his eyes welling up, and suddenly I remember who I am.

I am the mother, the one who can stop in the middle of a contraction, and I purposely reembody this role.

Arm in arm, Dante and I make our way to the car. Exhausted and traumatized, we allow this new reality to sink in, but with every fiber of my being, I wish I could take it all away.

This could have been all so different. We silently acknowledge this, and a surreal atmosphere encompasses us.

As the tale unfolds, we learn that the traffic suddenly backs up. Dante is following too close. He swerves into the empty lane, over-corrects, and makes contact with the rigid concrete barrier. This sends his car rolling across the highway, landing on the tires in the dusty median.

No substances are involved, or miraculously, any other vehicles. He is returning home from a long week of work in Pasadena. A few good Samaritans follow his truck into the dirt, jump out and race towards the burning car. These are the kind of people whom God enlists because they are more concerned with what will happen to their neighbor if they do not help than their own safety, and perhaps that is our most important calling.

It blew the windshield and windows out, and he can hear them yelling, "Get out of the car. Get out of the car."

The door is jammed, so he attempts to crawl through the window with flames flickering about the engine. They reach for him and lift him out, bleeding from several wounds but able to walk. They race across the freeway, dodging scattered debris, away from the burning car and the gas tank that's about to explode.

His guardian angel was working overtime, and for that, I am forever grateful.

They hand Dante water and a clean shirt to stanch the blood flowing from the wound on his head. An undercover cop pulls over and attempts to control the traffic. Within minutes, the cops roll up, along with several fire trucks and an ambulance. They retrieve his wallet, some cash, and a broken iPhone from the doused and damaged vehicle. Everything else turns to ash.

They secured the scene as Dante is loaded onto a gurney, and his sweet paramedic Jamie attempts to contact his family. Thank God he thought to contact Notre Dame, or it may have been hours before we knew what had happened to our son.

He leaves the hospital with a few staples in his head, stitches on his arm, and several bruises, but I have a feeling he harbors wounds that will never heal.

Our next stop is the wrecking yard. It's after hours, but they graciously let us rummage through the wreckage. We are shocked by the condition of the car and the realization that his survival was indeed miraculous. Life can profoundly turn on small choices. I say slow down, give each other space. Arrival is the goal, not the capricious passage of time or unexpected delays.

I don't care if the time passes quickly or slowly because I'm no longer dangling from the hands of a clock. I've become ensconced, held. Time now passes in unison with my beating heart.

Dante is exhausted, but I can't take my eyes off him as if he was a newborn, and I crawl into the back seat to sit next to him. I glance at his handsome profile. He's grown into such a kind-hearted, compassionate young man. Loyal, hardworking, and truly a blessing not only to our family but to our world. I'm fully aware each of us lives on borrowed time, and I plan on cherishing every minute with this one.

John O'Donohue says, "Everything we experience somehow passes into a past invisible place: when you think of yesterday and the things that were troubling you and worrying you, and the intentions that you had and the people that you met, and you know you experienced them all, but when you look for them now, they are nowhere—they have vanished..."

The destiny of all things is that they will disappear, but I believe gratitude is permanent and remains forever. This might be God's most compassionate grace.

DAVID CALVIN WOOD (1959 ~ 2019)

"My biggest worry is that when I'm dead and gone, my wife will sell my fishing gear for what I said I paid for it."
–Koos Brandtiggest

A missed call from your sister at 3:35 a.m. is never a good thing. Sitting up in bed, cradling the phone with shaking hands, I hesitate. There is this knowing, deep inside, that once I make this call, our lives will never be the same. So, I sit there, ashamed of my lack of courage, knowing she needs me. In my head, I'm screaming, "I don't want to know. I don't want to know."

That's when I hear my mom counseling me as if she were sitting right next to me. "Cheryl, she needs you. Honey, make the call." I finally comply. It's my mother. What else can I do?

With enormous dread, I tap the link from my favorites' file labeled sister. The minute I hear Nancy's mournful voice, "David passed," my countenance crumbles. I sink down into the bedding, hands covering my mouth. My cry is ragged and unrestrained. Tammy grabs the phone. As a nurse, she has been trained to remain calm in the most horrendous of situations. Her voice is soft but steady as she recounts the notable circumstances of the last few hours.

It was the middle of a cold, dark night when Nancy was awakened. Sleeping on the couch beside David, who fell asleep in the easy chair, she reaches over to wake him and bring him to bed. His face is cold. He is unresponsive. She calls 911.

Tammy arrives minutes after the paramedics, who desperately try to revive David, but he is already gone and, within the hour, they pronounced him dead.

The bereaved trio Nancy, Tammy, and Mackenzie are forced to say last goodbyes to a beloved husband and father as they enter uncharted territory, unprepared, shocked, and despairing. Clinging to one another so as not to be swept away by their raging emotions, they are left wondering how they will live without him.

"Most of the world is covered by water," says Charles Waterman. "A fisherman's job is simple: pick out the best spots." I would say David Calvin Wood was an overachiever. He also found the best woman, had two beautiful daughters, a precious grandson, and enjoyed the best life has to offer. He has a new heavenly birthday, January 25th, early morning, when all the good fishermen head out, his beloved wife by his side.

There are things death cannot touch. You know what I mean? Like the sound of his laughter, his distinctive footsteps ambling down the hall, the image of him sleeping in his easy chair, talking on the phone with Rick, pulling a fish out of the lake, and holding his grandson.

We never think of our time as finite. Instead, we saunter through life as if we will live forever. When the landscape of your life suddenly changes, you are left with the impossible task of repainting your life, minus the brilliant colors or familiar forms.

Why did he have to go in the middle of the night? Without warning. It's all so final. It no longer matters if you were embroiled in a saucy argument, harsh words left in mid-air, unfinished, never to be settled. This is life. It's as if a thief had broken into your heart and ransacked the chamber that stores your love. The damage is permanent and unretrievable.

Why weren't we paying closer attention? To everything: the way his eyes lit up when Nolan came over, his courage when tackling a multitude of health problems, how he wove a good story, his lifelong love of Disneyland, that crazy beard that tickled the ones he kissed, his contagious laugh, or how he looked forward to a meal with Nancy at Angelo's. Now we're forced to paste these memories together as if a collage without a border or frame.

She's left trying to reconcile all the David's she came to know, the one who kissed her after their first date with the one she kissed good night only days ago. I wonder if their first and last kiss is stirring in her soul.

I watch Nancy sitting listlessly in her chair. She looks small, lost, unaware of the chaos swirling around her. I know she's wondering how she will survive this incredible loss. She said to me, "How is it possible for someone with such a big presence to be here one minute and gone the next?"

I have no answers. It seems impossible, unjust, and inhumane. I realize people will lay their heads on their pillows tonight, with a loved one missing, and they will stare at the ceiling, the unused pillow, the robe still hanging on the bathroom door. Sleep will not visit them tonight as they're left wondering how they will survive this loss. Be kind to each other. We're all struggling with heavy burdens.

It's times like this that you are confronted with the past at every turn. His shoes still sit by the fireplace, the fishing poles leaning against the wall in the back of the garage, the half-empty glass of milk left on the counter. I read somewhere that grief is an existential testament to the worth of our beloved, to the way he was valued, to the love that was shared.

The relatives from Texas start arriving, as Vicky, Katie, Nathaniel, Carolina, and Violet ignore their own schedules, jump on a plane, and gather at the house to sit in "shiva" with Nancy as she mourns her beloved, along with David's cousins, Kathy, Rick, and Julie.

The thing about grief is you can't just get over it. It refuses to be shelved, forgotten, or put aside. Nicholas Wolterstorff says, "Every lament is a love song." I love that. Every lament is a love song to our beloved, a time to be cherished, shared, and revered in honor of this extraordinary man.

Daughters, Tammy and MacKenzie, are Nancy's anchors, holding her steady as relatives, friends, and neighbors rotate endlessly through the front door. With hugs, tears, and casseroles, we attempt to fill an inconceivable void. He was beloved. She is beloved, and together they made the world a better place. And as Ralph Waldo Emerson claims, "It is not length of life, but depth."

We're all looking for signs of David, like an unexplained breeze in a closed room, the whine of his hearing aid, the flicker of a light. We want to know he is with us. I find myself scanning the room in search of him until my eyes lock with my sisters, and we both know. He is with us.

Our primary calling is to love one another, so run to your beloved, kiss them on the lips, whisper in their ear, "I love you. I've loved you. I will always love you."

I'LL SEE YOU DOWN THE ROAD

"Mother is a word we use for an angel with wings of love."
–Apollo M

The view from my bed…

After watching an arresting movie last night, *Nomadland*, which left me feeling hollow and hallowed. I laid down with these intimate notions who spooned me as I dreamt. They were still with me in the early morning when the dew was fresh and the light sublime.

Hollow and hallowed are strange bedfellows, but the truth is that people can both struggle and remain upbeat simultaneously, through even the most soul testing of challenges, says Jessica Bruder.

After the death of my parents, I spent a lot of time with these emotions. I was completely wrecked but somehow comforted by a community who rallied around me as if numbers on a clock, reminding me, minute by minute, that I am not alone, that I am loved, that I can allow joy to spend time with my sorrow without feeling like a traitor.

"I don't ever say a final goodbye. I always just say, 'I'll see you down the road.'" Bob Wells.

When my sister struggled through the unexpected loss of her husband, I watched family and friends move in uninvited. We boarded her ailing vessel until the skin of our arms brushed up against one another and, although nothing can relieve this sort of pain, we rode those damn rapids together, and believe me when I say it was a class five river.

The most daring thing we do with our lives is to create community. This is our Great Barrier Reef against the waves of loneliness that can wash over us as if a tsunami in times of despair, but also when life is jubilant. It's a risk. You could be rejected, and if I were honest, I believe that is my deepest and most profound fear.

The premise of the movie *Nomadland* has to do with choiceless choices because often, we are forced to make important decisions in the throes of acute grief. We don't always participate in the circumstances that we find ourselves in, such as in the loss of a loved one, a marriage, job, friendship, pet, health, or even our integrity. Grief shows up without solicitation. It lingers like the smell of cologne on a borrowed jacket, the soundless cry in the back of our mind, estranged in the same body.

Having experience in each of these areas, I can empathize with the loss of a loved one, a fraught marriage (we all have our rocky moments), the ending of a job or career, a friendship that went south, a beloved dog that died, and the loss of integrity that can springboard off any of these deprivations. A poverty of spirit and hopelessness sets in, especially when we're anchored emotionally and financially to the past.

It's the people who show up in times of crisis that give us hope, who have the courage to sit with you in the darkness, not shedding light or speaking of their own loss. "The greatest gifts of all create space for the greatest sacrifices imaginable. For if we simply receive something that does not press us to give something in return, we will die fat with possessions but starved of meaning," says Craig D. Lounsbrough.

Love is a wonderful feeling, but the most basic form of love is action.

For me, heroes don't have to jump tall buildings or wear flashy capes. Their superpower lies in their ability to be present and to honor relationships over selfish desires. These are our first responders when tragedy hits. You know who you are, and I thank you.

My mother came to my rescue in this life more times than I care to count. She rescued me from not only bullies on the playground, injuries, and heartache but crying babies, friendships that didn't work out, and crushing failures. She stood with me in the face of insecurities, crippling doubt, and overwhelming fear. My mom was unrelenting when it came to her family. She was fiercely in my corner, and I could count on that like the rising of the sun. It changed me. It changed the way I move in the world because it's easy to be daring and brave when you know your warrior mama has your back.

The woman in this movie, Fern, decides to take her life on the road after losing her husband and her career. Even the town she lived in had died. She started following a group of nomads around the country as they vied for seasonal work as if they were modern-day migrants. "Many of the workers I met in the Amazon camps were part of a demographic that in recent years has grown with alarming speed: downwardly mobile older Americans," observes Jessica Bruder.

Of course, this made me think about my sister and my mom, both widowed at young ages, and both struggled to figure out how to live alone in a world designed for duos, but fortunately, they were anchored by homes and financial stability. For this, I am ever so grateful. According to 2015 census figures, among older women living alone, more than one in six are living below the poverty line. I am enormously happy my sister remains seven minutes from door to door, not wheel to wheel.

Jessica Bruder says, "... there is hope on the road. It's a by-product of forward momentum. A sense of opportunity, as wide as the country itself. A bone-deep conviction that something better will come." According to The New York Times Magazine, living in a van or van dwelling is fashionable.

The things we will do to escape from empty futures are as vast and creative as our human capacity to envision an alternative fate. You know what I mean?

Life on the road is physically taxing. The living space is claustrophobic. Driving long distances can be challenging, especially when you're alone and the gas is expensive. But the open road has its appeal, stopping on a whim, taking time to see the country up close, and enjoy the eccentric community of nomads you encounter along the way.

The thing is, we are proficient at finding places where we can pull off the road of life. Where we can rest, you might live in the city or on a quiet suburban street. You might find your rest at a truck stop amid the sound of idling engines. But as soon as the sun rises, before the neighbor retrieves her paper from the driveway, you're back on the road, moving on, secure in the knowledge that in this life and the next, you will find your place of rest.

As I open my bleary eyes this morning, spooned between hollow and hallowed, I'm transfixed by the window framing my view of the patio. Twinkling in the morning sun is a divine set of angel wings.

I whisper, "I'll see you down the road, mama."

LIFE IS TERMINAL

"When you reach your middle age, you see a train far away and shortly after you watch that train passing rapidly in front of you and finally the train disappears in the horizon like a streak of lightning! And that train, my dear friend, is your life!"
—Mehmet Murat ildan

Racing into the train terminal, I know time is of the essence. I see them clear as day. They're holding hands but appear lost.

After running the space of a basketball court, I greet my very deceased but surprisingly present mom and dad.

The next thing I know, I'm standing next to dad. He's older than I remember, but just as robust.

I realize I only have a few minutes. He's holding a long narrow ticket, but I can't identify the destination.

Where he's going doesn't matter, because I know he has something to say.

I sense its importance.

He leans in and whispers into my ear. I strain to catch every word.

He has always had this ability to change my narrative, the one I carry around with me, the one I hold up to everything else. This is his talent. He could turn me in a new direction faster than Amazon can deliver.

I'm beginning to realize this truth does not change because he's resting in an urn up at the lake house.

It's time. A gigantic locomotive pulls up to the platform. I reach for him, desperate for a hug before he returns from whence he came.

As I wake, the dream quickly fades, replaced by the stark reality — life is terminal.

This is the reality under which we all live.

I glance at the clock on the nightstand.

It's 6:05 a.m.

December 16, 2019.

Nine years to the minute since my dad passed away.

I lay there trying to remember what he said, but deep down, I know.

He's worried.

And he wants me to remember who I am.

I lean back in bed. Across the room, my ghostly reflection wavers on the French doors that frame the courtyard. The light is shifting from inky darkness to a muted gray.

With the dawning of the day comes the realization that my dad has indeed shifted my narrative from the grave.

I remember that flight to Washington (almost a decade ago) as if it were yesterday. It was early morning on the 16th of December when Nancy called to alert me of Dad's death.

He died hours before I was to arrive in the Northwest.

With tears streaming down my face the entire flight, I think everyone around me was relieved when the plane landed, and they no longer had to endure the howling of the hysterical woman in seat 22b.

I grab my bag and race to the arrival gate OJ Simpson style.

Frantically searching the cars for her familiar face.

I finally see her rounding the bend, weaving through the traffic as if George Costanza pushing a frogger down the street.

She pulls up to the curb and jumps out of the car with the engine still running.

I'm in her arms, hysterical, holding tight, and for a moment, my world stops spinning.

My sister has always been my anchor, especially in times of need.

She is my rock.

Our hearts are not functioning properly, but together, breathing seems plausible.

She finally steps away, hands me a tissue and the keys.

"You're driving."

That's sort of our modus operandi.

She navigates. I drive, and this is how we've managed thus far.

We gathered up our mama that very same day and brought her home.

It was our highway of tears as we drove 753 miles down I5 from Chehalis to Campbell.

Speaking almost no words, we stopped for coffee and more tissues.

Mom was shattered, empty. The word bereft was not adequate to describe her state of being.

This is how death scars one's soul, because how is it possible to restore a vessel once it is so completely broken?

Band-Aids hold it together, but as if a stigmata, it continues to bleed.

It felt much the same, early morning on the 25th of January, racing to Nancy's house, devastated by the news my beloved brother-in-law had passed away.

It was still dark outside. We sat huddled around the fire, sipping coffee, tears flowing, watching the sunrise.

Surreal is one word that comes to mind.

What alarmed me most was the vacantness in her eyes, as if being present was too much to bear. I thought I knew grief, but this was different.

This is why he came.

She's finding it difficult to navigate, and he wants me to provide transport.

I'm here, sweet sister. I'm right here.

PART IV: PROVISIONAL

CAN I TELL YOU ABOUT MY DAY?

"The job of every generation is to discover the flaws of the one that came before it. That's part of growing up, figuring out all the ways your parents and their friends are broken."
–Justine Larbalestier

Good, because if I don't let it out, it's going to escape in some other form and, at my age, excessive flatulence is unbecoming.

By midday, I had written Extra Strength Tylenol on the grocery list three times.

Most of you will agree that sheltering in place is wearing on our collective nerves, and today was another of many. Too many to count. Bahaha, I'm so dramatic, but it makes for a good story, so read on...

Their arrival was as if an ant invasion, massive, unstructured, and unrelenting. Julie, my oldest daughter, is having work done in her house, so her family is sheltering with us. Keep in mind all the adults are working remotely. There are three children under the age of five who need care. Two are identical twins, and my dog is sick as a dog.

Julie arrives with Audrey, her oldest, sporting a five-year-old pirated royalty attitude. It's fricken adorable. Cora and Sienna, now three, are courting mischievous grins. Enough said. They make a beeline for the dress-up trunk in the mermaid room while Nic sets up his home office on the kitchen table, right across from Julie's refrigerator-accessible office. Does everyone really need a computer, a huge monitor, a snaggle of cords, and important-looking papers?

Where am I supposed to eat breakfast?

I just finished a five-mile trek through the neighborhood with Sue (six feet apart, of course) and needed strong coffee, a boiled egg, and a restroom. The rough restaurant-style toilet paper has made me appreciate the good old days when we stocked Charmin Ultra Soft in the bathrooms, and the "experience" could be described as pleasant. Today, I feel as if someone has taken a sander to my ass. Rough. [update: after reading this, my neighbor Chris came running across the street with a 6-pack of Charmin Ultra Soft. This is why I blog.]

They brought the babysitter with them, Ms. Hilda, whom I found sitting on the playroom floor, tying elaborate bows around the girls' fashionable dresses, as they scampered about securing jewelry and purses. There was an intense squabble developing over the turquoise necklace, so I hastened to the kitchen before they dragged me in.

Larry, Nic, and Julie are all on conference calls, of course, AirPods protruding from their important ears. They're trying to communicate with me via frantic eye movements, which are annoying. Who the hell is fluent in eye movements? I speak in a loud and clear voice so as not to be misunderstood. "Move over. You're blocking the coffee pot." I get the look.

I don't know why I bother saying this over and over again, "Please remember to put your dishes in the dishwasher, hence the name. The sink is full. You've been here less than an hour and try to remember it's May." I get those frantic hand signals to cease and desist with my rant, but I'm avoiding eye contact, so I can't hear you!

I realize it's hard to tell, but it is May, my birthday month, and not that I'm expecting to be worshiped (much) or anything, but at least tolerated!

Racing past the playroom door to avoid exposure, I slip into the master bedroom to set up my "home office." Okay, I slap on Airpods just to look cool, even though my conference call isn't until tomorrow. Wasn't it Jesus who said, "Preparedness is next to Godliness."? Maybe that was my mother? Anyhoo... I am late posting my blog. I have absolutely nothing to say, and it's hell to expand on nothing. I also have eleven students who need help with their summative projects, a workshop to attend, and a dog who appears to be dying.

Did I mention I wrote Extra Strength Tylenol on the grocery list three times?

The doorbell rings. It's Leticia, our beloved housekeeper. We've been paying her not to come for the last two months, but she's ready to work again and asked if she could start today. Perfect, it's no longer possible to stay 6 feet apart in my own house. I invite her in and try to rationalize all the people camped in various rooms. I guess we'll just have to evacuate the areas where she's cleaning. It's called herd control, something to do with immunities. I mean mobility.

Oh yes, the dog, let me fill you in on his impending death. It could be an entire chapter, but I'll give you the abridged version. You're welcome. For reasons unknown, he licked the fur off his back paw while we were at the lake last weekend. He can't put any weight on it, and he's resistant to inspections. Larry and I finally tackled him together on the carpet and found a stinger embedded in the sensitive part of his now bare toe (or is it a claw?). Anyway, we graciously removed it. But he keeps licking the sore spot, and now it's not only hairless but infected. Larry has duct-taped an old sock over the entire foot, and that seemed to work until yesterday, when we discovered he wasn't able to put weight on the opposing front paw. So now, he's like an unstable table and has to be carried everywhere, and for the first time ever, he's not interested in food?

He's garnering a lot of attention. It's my birthday month, but I believe I'm managing it all quite well. Thank you for asking.

Shaggy has been glued to my side for days. He does this when he's feeling poorly, and I believe everyone is a little jealous. Could it be my own projection? Who knows?

Regardless, I have an eighty-pound rug constantly underfoot. I've tripped at least a dozen times, and I may have broken my pinky toe.

Did I mention I wrote Extra Strength Tylenol on the grocery list three times?

Shaggy can't maneuver through his dog door with two useless feet, which have forced Larry into resistant servitude, and as you would expect, Larry's back went out during my birthday month, and he's a little cranky, just sayin'.

I'm very worried, as one would imagine. Who's going to make my coffee?

Shaggy has an appointment this morning with the vet, so Larry recruited Dante to go with him and do the heavy lifting. As they carried our very matted and ungroomed Shaggy to the car, Larry could not stop himself from saying, "You might never see him again. Say your goodbyes." This announcement created a lot of unnecessary drama, moaning, and lamenting, but soon the AirPods went back into the ears, Leticia back to dusting, and the children have rather short attention spans.

Audrey tired of dress-up after three minutes and decided she wanted to be a writer like her Grammie. What can you do? I need to finish my blog. It's Thursday. I'm already a day late. Setting Audrey up with an old laptop, I pulled up a blank Google document and found an old skateboard, which I repurposed as a desk. Then I typed the vowels at the top of the page and told her to make up words using consonants and at least one vowel. Bad idea.

This is how it went down.

"Grammie, what is this word?"

"Eget."

"What does it mean?"

I look it up and read her the definition: "eget, adverb, personally, individualistically, uniquely, oddly, peculiarly." Reminds me of my life.

Two seconds later, "Grammie, what is this word?"

"Gnat."

"What does it mean?"

"It could be a small bug that hangs out in large swarms or a person seen as tiny or insignificant, especially in comparison with something larger or more important." Hum, strangely appropriate.

I tell her to write a lot of words, and then we'll look at them all together. I haven't written one sentence on my blog. Who can think with all these words to define?

Two seconds later, "Grammie, what is this word?"

I ignore the comment.

"GRAMMIE, WHAT IS THIS WORD?"

"Grammie is trying to write, honey."

"This word!"

Ugg, "Dolt."

Did I mention I wrote Extra Strength Tylenol on the grocery list three times?

When the veterinarian calls with the results of Shaggy's condition, we crowd around Larry's iPhone as if some juicy gossip was about to be revealed. Even the housekeeper moves within range. Shaggy is not going to die. He had burrs in both paws from all the ungroomed hair and lake life. Total dog fail. Larry and Dante go back to the vet to retrieve him. He comes home with this huge cone attached to his head, so he doesn't continue to lick the infected paws. He's not adjusting well to the new impediment, knocking into doors and walls, and he can't reach his water bowl. If this seems comical, it's because it is, and I'm an evil person.

When Julie gets done with her conference calls, she saunters into my hastily constructed office, where I'm getting absolutely nothing done. "I won't be able to cook at my house tonight. What are you feeding us for dinner?" Wonderful, my clean kitchen will be a faint memory by evening's end. Oh, joy.

"We were going to have salmon."

"That sounds great."

"Let me call Dante. He's at the store. We'll be needing a bigger fish."

I text Dante, "The ants are staying for dinner. Buy some bait!"

As soon as Dante returns, I start prepping the fish, beets, salad, and broccoli. I plan on roasting everything but the salad. The kiddos are hanging on me like piranhas. Audrey is following me around, asking about words, and the dog remains underfoot. Deep breaths, a wee bit of wine, "Honey, did you remember the Tylenol?

I move to the family room to wait for the water to boil. The entourage moves with me. "Audrey, please don't run on the back of the couch. It's not a balance beam, and Cora, sweetheart, don't drive the camper repeatedly into the piano. Shaggy, stop licking. Has anyone seen Sienna?" In fact, where is everyone?

As the pot of water starts to boil for the kids' pasta, I notice a contingent of neighbors gathering in our driveway. Larry, Dante, Julie, and Nic are all out there shooting the shit, sipping adult beverages. I yell out the window, "Six feet, people," just to be ornery. Hello, we're in the middle of a pandemic, not a continual happy hour, and by the way, my glass is empty. Did I mention it's my birthday month and I'm the only one in the kitchen?

I send the kids and the unstable table (a.k.a. Shaggy) out front. Tahehehe!

During dinner, I watch the twins draw pictures with the butter on their pink plastic plates with their fingers. I look the other way, but when Audrey reapplies her lipstick with my favorite color, I calmly retrieve it and stick it in my bra for safekeeping. "Can we excuse the children, please"?

Corralling them all into the tub is like herding cats, but eventually, we succeed.

Sienna says, "I a mermaid. Do you like my tail, Grammie?" She holds her legs together and slams them up and down in the water.

"I love your tail, but please stop splashing water all over my freshly cleaned bathroom."

"Grammie, I a mermaid."

Who knew how precocious all those tiny butts could be? One of them farts.

"For Heaven's sake, what's that noise?"

"What noise, Grammie?" Giggles.

"That horrible smelly noise."

"What did it sound like?" More giggles.

"You didn't hear it?"

"No." Collective giggles.

"Never mind. Just stop. You'll poop in the tub."

Let me just say poop happens.

You have to wonder what they will remember from this Corona experience? It won't be the adults scrambling to work remotely, the tension of isolation, or fear of the unknown. They'll tell their children about dinners at Grammie's, spending half the day in their pajamas, birthday parties in the driveway, homemade corona masks from Kiki, but maybe, the most important remembrance is all the time they spent with mom and dad.

Thanks for letting me emit this story as if releasing gas from a chamber. I feel relieved.

GIVE IT A REST

"People say nothing is impossible, but I do nothing every day,"
–A.A. Milne, Winnie-the-Pooh

I have been living under flagrantly false assumptions my entire life. I do not know how in tarnation this happened. And to make matters worse, I discovered this inanity by accident. Normally I'd call my mother to rant, but that's not possible. Is it really a revelation if you don't share it?

I didn't think so, so I wrote it all down. You're welcome.

The truth is, I'm a natural sloth who has been sipping the Kool-Aid of work-a-holics for far too long. Resting gets a bad rap, and I'm here to repackage this preposterous vilification. People can be so judgmental. If you don't want to feel guilty every time you put your damn feet up, then please read on…

I've been running at breakneck speeds for nearly half a century, trying to keep up with the Jones whom I barely know. If this pandemic has taught me a thing or two, I'm not a shark, and I won't die if I stop all motion; and two, the Jones, who have never even invited me to dinner, have way too much influence on our cultural expectations. During this perpetual lockdown, I found time to be a gift, as in the present moment, the one I'm standing in, and by the way, time could care less if I'm mopping the floor or lounging in the recliner.

I'm going to ask you to do something rather uncomfortable. Stop with the whining. It's not like I'm asking for money.

For experiential purposes, you'll need to reposition yourself before reading any further. It's pivotal, so don't skip this part because you may think God is not watching, but She is, and your collaboration has been noted.

Idleness is not the root of all evil, as the Jones would have you think. It is the fertilizer that is required if you wish to *Grow, Damn It*.

It's imperative that your brain be aligned with your body, so find a lounge chair, a bed, the floor, and maybe a couple of pillows to elevate your feet. Shoes off, obviously. A blanket is essential, like after yoga class, and if you can repurpose your face mask to shelter your eyes, that would be swell. Send me a pic because I know your phone is within arm's reach.

Personally, I like a cup of coffee no further than eight inches from my nose. That's just me. Consider that optional.

This is called lounging. It takes a few minutes to get used to the idea. Like grief, don't rush the process. Stay put until your thoughts settle down, your brain chills, and you are no longer cognizant of the chatter going on around you. Remember to breathe. We inhale and exhale the same way we hang on to worries and let them go.

And please ignore any despairing comments about your comportment from roommates. Stay the course. Those people are under the influence of the Jones and not in their right mind.

After a half hour or so, you'll stop noticing the dusty baseboards, suspicious stains on the carpet, and dead flies decomposing under the coffee table. You'll be tempted to get up and grab a dust rag. Dissent like a Ginsburg. Dust does not expire.

This is harder than it looks. You need to wear down your restlessness. Consider this a well-deserved sabbatical. I read that Albert Einstein pondered the riddle of the universe with a cat on his lap. And wasn't Isaac Newton sitting under a tree when he came up with the law of universal gravitation? I mean, with your ass anchored to the ground, it seems elementary, but it was clever.

We can't solve problems we haven't yet identified, and if you find yourself meditating on the nature of upholstered furniture, stay prone. This is critical. God only knows what issues you'll resolve with new *material* to work with.

We all know someone who likes nothing better than to check things off their to-do list, tag the finish line (Sue Goudreau), complete a task, or they feel out of sorts, stifled, or suppressed. It's ridiculous, and I'm determined to help you with the initial readjustments. Henry David Thoreau says, "Disobedience is the true foundation of liberty."

Let your mind meander. It's like eating the forbidden fruit. I'm talking the biblical kind, but you don't have to worry about your nakedness. Think about the way rivers meander throughout the land. We don't know why, but they take us places we never thought we would go. Think Huckleberry Finn: "We said there warn't no home like a raft, after all. Other places do seem so cramped up and smothery, but a raft don't. You feel mighty free and easy and comfortable on a raft."

One more thing, do not schedule your idleness, then it just becomes another obligation. Be spontaneous with your play. We've been sheltering in place for the better part of a year. If you haven't figured out how to be a vagabond at home, then you're missing out. Seriously.

It is perfectly fine to abandon activities midstream. Don't get all sanguine about it. Just walk away. I do this all the time. As I'm organizing the bananas in the fruit bin, I find myself drawn to the window that's streaked with three years of life. I shrug, throw some dishcloths on the hardwood, and skate up and down the hall to Frank Sinatra. Ten minutes later, I'm hunting for lost car keys when I stumble on a drawer of maps and decide to alphabetize them. Maybe I'll call my sister. She's working and likes to be disrupted.

I have it on good authority that an hour of procrastination is equivalent to an hour at the gym. It's the resistant training that makes all the difference. Get it?

You can strengthen your resolve to remain idle by looking at something that needs attending to. A sink full of dishes is my lifelong nemesis. Feel the tension build as you ignore the impulse to amend the situation. Fight it. Grab a bowl of pistachios if you need support. After a few weeks, you'll be amazed at the fortitude of your resistance, not to mention the increased finger dexterity and fiber consumption. There's the bloom.

Don't let the feudal establishment deter you. There is more to happiness than rigid schedules, impressive resumes, and a fat paycheck (well, maybe that).

For most of us, "not doing" is just about the most difficult thing anyone could ask of us. We've been searching for that elusive something that remains just out of reach because the Jones keep moving the damn target. Rest is not optional. It's required for a strong sense of well-being. To sit in your favorite chair and sip coffee or lie on the grass under the shade of a tree listening to a crow squawk is a radically counter-cultural act in the modern world.

Maybe we've been wrongly informed about the purpose of life?

Most spiritual leaders claim peace of mind is the ultimate goal and, apparently, it's always attainable. Jesus described it as prayer. Muhammad preached submission. Buddha suggested detachment, but all encouraged contemplative practices, avoiding secular seductions and cycles of cravings. They can't all be wrong?

The charade is over. I will never be a perfect being, and counting my mishaps is counterproductive, but while I was relaxing, I discovered that unexceptional is extraordinary enough. Maybe it's high time we recapture our penchant for idleness, stop labeling everything we do, and just give it a rest!

NOT THAT YOU ASKED

"Before you were conceived, I wanted you. Before you were born, I loved you. Before you were an hour, I would die for you. This is the miracle of love."
–Maureen Hawkins

I believe a family update is in order as I am recovering from last week's post-traumatic stress, and I could use a little support from things that don't slither or build webs.

Even gratuitous interest is welcome.

As you know, my daughter Julie, son-in-law Nic, and three granddaughters have been living with us for the better part of a year as they unabashedly stole our contractor so they could remodel their recently purchased house across the street.

Then my other daughter, Kelley, and her husband, Tim, arrived from Boston for an extended stay because that's what you do when there's a pandemic. You bubble. My youngest son Dante has never moved out.

If you're so inclined, send sympathy cards with lottery tickets.

Something I knew but conveniently forgot over time: three-year-old's scream. A lot. It's sort of an ear-piercing howl that lingers in the air as if a recently smoked cigar. You know what I mean? But so do their giggles, and that's the win.

I wake up to the echo of soft laughter coming from down the hall and can't remember a time when this wasn't so.

The odd thing is, when it's quiet, you know there's trouble brewing. That's when you jump up and rush the tranquility.

Rounding the corner to the room in which the twins were last seen, I ask accusingly, "What are you two doing?"

"Nothing (in unison)," claims Cora and Sienna, looking up at me with the most cherubic faces you have ever seen.

"What's in your hands?"

Four sets of little hands disappear. "Nothing, Grammie."

"Are those Kiki's earrings I see scattered all over the floor, dangling from your shirt, hiding in your hands?"

"We organizing, Grammie."

"Did Kiki ask you to organize her jewelry?"

"Yes, she did," says Cora.

"Seems odd?"

"We helping," says Sienna, as she holds a crystal earring up to her ear.

"Let's put them all back, and then we can have an Otter Pop!"

By the way, Otter Pops solve everything.

Can we move on to the industriousness of our five-year-old roomie? When this child is in pursuit of an important task, it is nearly impossible to dissuade her. Recently I found her creating a collage with my latest DIY magazine. Later that day, she was using my toothbrush as her own after relocating my lipsticks to an undisclosed location. Today she was lavishing my French perfume on the dog, and my hair clip has mysteriously disappeared.

It's quite possible Shaggy not only smells but looks better than the humans with whom he resides.

And by the way, adult children revert to their adolescent personas when in the company of their parents. Only now, they're educated, self-funded, and not subject to parental restrictions or grounding.

It's utter mayhem.

Even so, everyone is getting their needs met, albeit with a few peculiar compromises and silent negotiations. We're under construction, literally and metaphorically. When Julie and Nic took ownership of the house across the street, it needed serious renovations, but that's the beauty of a large family. "Many hands make light work," John Heywood notes.

Families have their own micro-culture. It's as if a bustling harbor, a place to moor your person while you recover from the stress of the outside world. Love makes the ride worthwhile, and family is your fast pass.

The best part of being in a large family is you don't have to waste your time trying to prove yourself in order to be loved. We care about each other, value one another's opinion, even when we're acting like total assholes. At least we take turns.

Can I just add some of us have taken more turns than others? As Jonathan Carroll reminds us: "Real love is always chaotic. You lose control; you lose perspective. You lose the ability to protect yourself. The greater the love, the greater the chaos." It's a given, and that's the secret.

I have learned through long, and convoluted discussions that disagreements don't get resolved. They hibernate until a new issue emerges, and they return disguised as concern, judgment, or control. There are no winners in the ring of unresolved conflict, just knockouts and bruised feelings. You can't change people. It's more about acceptance and the resolve to agree to disagree. I need to learn to be okay with that, move on, and grab an Otter Pop.

Here's another hiccup when you live in crowded conditions with wannabe fairies, aka Cora, Sienna, and Audrey. Things get lost! Julie lost a wallet. Larry couldn't find his keys or flip-flops, and I believe there was a necklace that went missing for several days. I keep losing the book I'm currently reading. Our shoes are never where we left them, and we are always in search of our iPhones. When one phone rings, seven people go into a hard scramble—and one of them doesn't even own a phone?

One day, I was using my Airpods, and the next day they were gone! I accused everyone (including Shaggy) of borrowing them and then failing to return the merchandise. They all vehemently denied any knowledge of their whereabouts (keep in mind the four of us have the exact same model).

A week later, I found them precisely where I always store them and had searched this location no less than fifteen times! Fairies or adults? We'll never know for sure.

As soon as the kids got the keys to their new house; we migrated across the street, forming this makeshift crew of amateur artists attempting to paint a new portrait over a previously used canvas. Plans have been submitted to the city for an extensive remodel, and while they await approval, there is a lot of prep work that needs to be done. The first order of operations was to pull up all the old carpet, clean out the garage for storage, remove the draperies and rods, along with some of the landscaping, and finally take down the dated wallpaper.

It's interesting to me how our lives follow the same cycles. We experience periods of creation followed by deconstruction and then reconstruction, and it's the same for houses, cultures, governments, movements, relationships, and even our faith. Is this what you think about when you can't sleep? I didn't think so.

Too bad we're deconstructing this beautiful house in the middle of July. It's hot and humid, and I believe I have sweated out half my body weight, pulling carpet staples out of the floorboards.

As luck would have it, our beloved cousin Vicky is visiting from Texas, she's staying with my sister, and the two of them stopped by with pliers to help remove staples from the floors. We all ended up sitting in my driveway around 5:00 pm and opened some chilled Sauvignon Blac to quench our thirst. It's this, the memories of working together to bring about each other's dreams, that makes life so damn sweet.

We were delighted to find unexpected hardwood under all the carpets, solid wood doors in all the rooms, and a wallpaper mural of Paris in the dining room! Everywhere I look, I sense a surfeit of memories and traditions lodged in the walls of this charming house and smile warmly at the sweet memories domiciled in the future.

Our lives are continually under construction. Just when things get comfortable, we redesign the idle spaces. "Every day, we reconstruct ourselves out of the salvage of our yesterday's," says James Sallis. I say family is but a glimpse of heaven simmering on the fires of hell, and as Olaf says, some people are worth melting for.

THE LETTERS

"To write is human, to get mail: Divine!"
–Susan Lendroth

I didn't know it would be the last letter I would ever write my mother, that it would never be delivered, and I would not discover it until four years after her death.

Have you ever questioned your understanding of time? How it slips by unnoticed until one day we're given a blatant reminder, the meter is ticking on our lives, reminding us not to waste a single moment.

My reminder came right from the grave.

As you know, there's a story behind everything. Sometimes the stories are simple, and sometimes they are humorous, but behind most of my stories is my mother because she is the beginning, middle, and end of me.

I share this story enmeshed in deep emotions that have nowhere to go but onto the page. Receive it gently, with the utmost care. I'm a fragile one today.

There is no way around it. I need to clean out my grandmother's desk in preparation for the blasted remodel, and I've been procrastinating for weeks. Okay, months. Seriously. The tasks I allow to get between me and this old desk range from dusting the ceiling fans and spit shining the kitchen faucet to scrubbing the latrines.

What am I avoiding?

Dust, tarnish, and grim? No!

I'm afraid of confronting all those potent memories tucked in that broken-down, antiquated secretary with four innocent-looking wooden drawers. It's my Pandora's box because, over the years, it has become my favorite place to stash that which I love but have no place.

It's where I stored all the crap from my stamp phase. I used to ink everything with *Have a nice day* and smiley faces. Nothing was sacred, not letters, lunch bags, or the back of one's hand. Thank God it was only a phase. There are at least a dozen manuscripts of my first novel in various stages of completion, all bound, covered, and dated. Along with stacks of old report cards, an old farmhouse calendar my sister gave me when we lived in Kansas, catechism projects, flashlights, cords dating back to the last century, gift certificates, sunglasses in various stages of disrepair, stationery for every occasion, decades of Mother's Day cards, coupons I never redeemed, even an eyeglass repair kit. Oh, and a couple of fans you plug into a computer from my menopausal days.

I know. I know. I'm a hoarder, but I'm coming out of the desk (so to speak), and into the light. As I sift through years of rubbish, I notice my proclivities surfacing as if the sun in the early dawn.

So I have my keeper box sitting on the floor next to my chair, and I decide to work from the bottom drawer up. I've discarded just about everything in every drawer, except for the calendar my sister gave me because now it appears charming, and I think it will be adorable in the mermaid room.

I toss all the old manuscripts, except for the latest version, the entire stamp collection, along with the dried-up ink pads, fans, flashlights, walkie-talkies, and felt pens that have long since dried. It's like losing weight. You never want to go through the privation again, but the result is delightful.

The area I'm actively avoiding is the pull-down section of the desk. This is the easiest place to stash things quickly, especially when unexpected guests arrive at the door. I would dump whatever seemed unsightly in this cavernous vault, but consistently failed to retrieve the embarrassing clutter when the commotion died down. Well, I don't know about you. That's just me. I'll deal with it later, is my go-to motto.

Lining the back of the desk is a built-in section with two secret pocket storage cubbies and a bunch of open cubicles that are completely jammed with God knows what untidy things.

As I open the desk, we exhale together, as if the desk and I are experiencing the same deflating emotions. I would take just about any excuse not to spend the next hour of my dwindling life evaluating the remains of this mysterious formation of catacombs if you will.

Slumping in the chair, I try to mentally prepare for the task ahead. I'll need coffee, for sure. My feet are cold, and I owe my sister a call.

See, any excuse.

Grabbing the contents out of the first cubby, I sift through stacks of crinkled papers. One is a grocery list for Christmas dinner, some recipe cards for various traditional dishes (all available online), a few receipts from Target, Safeway, CVS, and a note reminding me to schedule the dog for grooming. In the second section, note pads, old key rings, six two-dollar bills I was going to put in the kids' Easter eggs but forgot, and these beautiful red envelopes I ordered on Amazon. What the hell was I thinking? Most of it gets tossed, keeping the two-dollar bills and red envelopes, which I'll forget about next year, and God willing, I'll find them again when I'm 80.

Several cubbies later, I'm completely exhausted. This is worse than working out or plucking my eyebrows. I check the secret drawers. There's a note reminding me where I hid mom's silver, brilliant. I only spent a year searching the house for the missing cutlery. In the center is a cupboard that locks. I find the key inside attached to a rabbit's foot. Lucky me.

As I'm quickly sifting through the last of the stalls, my hand lands on a stack of bright green envelopes, all sealed and labeled. I hold them in my hand for a minute. What the hell are these? One is for my sister, one for Sue, Phyllis, Mary, and Jill. The last one is labeled mom.

A jolt of emotion runs through me. She was alive when I wrote this.

Taking the stack to my room, I set them on mom's marble table. I'm not ready. I realize I'm holding a piece of my mom that, once revealed, will no longer feel like an encounter, and this is what I want more than anything.

It occurs to me, as if Scarlett O'Hara. "After all, tomorrow is another day."

Refreshing my coffee, I sit in the chair and stare at the notes as if they were the blessed Eucharist and the presence of each person is resting with me. We're having dinner with the Bahue's in a few days, so I can deliver Phyllis' note in person. We have dinner plans with the Armstrong's scheduled in a week or two, and I will see Mary and Jill at that event. I'll bring Sue's on our walk tomorrow, and Nancy's the next time I join her for coffee.

Maybe we'll be able to figure out by the content of the message when they were written?

Over the next several weeks, I pass out the notes to my friends and sister, where we discover they are indeed thank-you notes for birthday gifts from five years ago. I was deeply invested in mom's care by that time and must have stuck them on the desk, hoping to post them when I had some time. But they were forgotten in the fog of caring for someone who was laboring from this life to the next.

Weeks pass, and the little note with the word mom sits on the table in my bedroom, as if I was going to see her soon and can pass it along. As I've noted before, it's not a good idea to get between me and my delusions. There it sits, taunting me to pick it up, to read the words, to remember a time when I had the privilege of thanking her for the many ways she gifted my life.

Finally, I'm alone in our home, a rarity these days, with her little green note. I pick up the envelope, gauge the weight of it in my hand, turning it over and over while trying to imagine what I might have been thinking when I sat down to write her this last note when I thought I could just pop in the mail, and she'd receive it days later.

Slipping my finger between the flap and the envelope, dislodging the old glue, I gently pull out the folded note.

Dearest Mom...

I linger with the words of gratitude, thanking my sweet mom for the last birthday gift she would ever purchase for me. I think of the courage it took for her to battle this hideous disease and how in the world she found the energy to think of me on my birthday. In this last note, I express my love and my gratitude. I write of her heroic fight, and dare to speak of her next birthday, the one time did not allow us to celebrate.

Holding back tears, I'm overwhelmed with unshed emotion.

Who could have known that I would read these words from the past when the person I am today no longer has a mother?

If there were an eleventh commandment, my mom would have added, thou shall write a thank you note for every gift ever received. If I failed to write my notes in a timely manner, I felt as if I needed to go to confession. Seriously.

How do you know when a hug will be your last? I did not know it was the last time I would hold her hand, the last time we would laugh together, the last moments I would spend with the woman who brought me into this world, connected umbilically, and yet, she continues to nourish me with unexpected gifts in the form of a card stashed in the cubby of her mother's desk, reminding me how grateful I am for her love.

Thank God because I would not have been able to function if I had known these were my last moments with the woman who raised me to write thank-you notes. Now I know why.

Whenever I don't know what to do with my wayward emotions, I call my sister.

"Hey, Nan," like a thousand calls before, but today I'm cognizant of our transience, and I store the memory in the cubby of my heart.

HONEY, I'M HOME FOREVER

"Often when you think you're at the end of something, you're at the beginning of something else. I've felt that many times. My hope for all of us is that 'the miles we go before we sleep' will be filled with all the feelings that come from deep caring—delight, sadness, joy, wisdom—and that in all the endings of our life, we will be able to see the new beginnings."
–Fred Rogers

I've been shot twice now, in the left arm, and I'm a little unsettled about life after vaccination. Additionally, I'm horrified to admit I've developed a mild case of agoraphobia over the last year—might have something to do with prolonged Zoom calls. It's a theory, baseless, really, but if not Zoom, then it's definitely *The Larry Factor*. The idea of planning a cruise, a dinner party, or a massage seems rather terrifying, maybe even irresponsible.

I've become a walking germaphobe, and honestly, the masks are only exasperating my condition.

We've been through a lot lately, both individually and collectively, so let's go easy on each other. I don't know about you, but I'm tired, tired of doing nothing but numbing the dread of the unknown for the better part of a year. And by the way, "trying" to be "happy" isn't getting rid of the angst. It's always there, a dull ache, the silver lining of my personal cumulus cloud.

The truth is I've been hibernating, as if a bear with a den of restless cubs, and I'm lethargic, okay grouchy, and fat (the PC term is fluffy). Seriously, I could do daily workouts with those insane Peloton instructors, and I'd still have a healthy layer of insulation that would get me through the next three winters. Try not to judge.

And not to complain, but my students are under some sort of spell. Try as I may to hook them with stellar lesson plans (Bahaha), I only manage to wake them up briefly before they slip back into their COVID comas and crawl under their hoodies.

I hope to wake up one morning and discover this was all just a dream.

Well, more like a nightmare, but let's focus on the positive.

Just when Larry and I have become addicted to endless hugs and kisses from our grandkids and the sound of laughter reverberating off the walls of our home, they pack up and leave. Our villages came so close together that I could no longer discern the beginnings and endings. Well, that and the fact they moved across the street.

As my cubs relocated, it's as if the house doubled in size, right down to the hallowed halls, and can I just say the silence is deafening? I'm not kidding. I have trained my ears to identify the sounds of distressed children for like a year as if I'm a massive sonar device, and now all I pick up is a noiseless void. It's unnerving.

The thing is, home is not the house, or the town in which you live. It's the people you love and the ones who love you, and it's not just when you get together. It's not a place but the experience of each other that creates a shelter as if bricks, one that you carry with you for your entire life, that's home.

Yesterday, I putzed around the house for like the first time in a year, adjusting the trinkets that survived my grandkids, fluffing pillows that will stay where I place them, and returning abandoned toys to the cupboards. I had a big decision to make, and I was wallowing in the ability to linger with my thoughts for more than a few minutes without disruption.

Not to complain, but our sleep patterns have become as erratic as the availability of toilet paper. By 8:00 p.m., we can no longer keep our eyes open (let's agree to agree it's not just about the wine), and then, for the life of us, we can't figure out why we're wide awake at 2:00 a.m. playing solitaire on our phones? Okay, I play solitaire. Larry searches YouTube for things like porcelain repair and how to get crayon art off textured walls.

I say it's the residual of a pandemic whose contagions have altered our internal clocks, possibly forever, or the house is haunted.

The next thing I know, Kelley and Tim show up on our doorstep the very day the guest room is vacated. Definitely a sight for sore eyes. I haven't seen them since their wedding last year!

Kelley's a Kondo kick ass, and now that both Julie's and my houses are in various states of disarray, we need some serious help. I have cleared out three gigantic cupboards, and a closet, and although I have miles to go, there are only a few weeks before our remodel begins. Keep in mind my deeply embedded aversion to change, and all these adjustments are taking a toll on my sense of well-being.

Chanting is an option? It doesn't work, but it annoys the roommates. And that's rather satisfying.

Julie and Nic now have a fully functioning kitchen, and we have given it a worthy christening. Nic has already cooked up some delicious gourmet hamburgers, savory eggs benedict, and an elegant chicken salad. He's a brilliant, overly generous chef, and I blame him for my evolving curvaceousness.

Drumroll, please... so here's my exciting news!

Today, I'm giddy to announce my retirement after 15 years at Notre Dame. I sent a note I've been holding in a draft folder for weeks to the principal, vice-principal, chair, and co-workers, informing them of my intention to retire at the end of this academic year. Instantly, I wanted to rescind the note, but I reminded myself about the champagne I bought for tonight's celebration and decided to resign myself to resigning. As my co-worker, Deidre, says, a bottle of champagne is an excellent motivator for SO MANY life choices. Pretty sure that's why they serve it at weddings.

We gathered around Julie's generous island to celebrate my newfound identity, or maybe my ability to make a damn decision. Kelley did one of those boomerang things as I popped the champagne and filled our glasses. She posted it on Instagram, and like half a dozen people messaged me to see if she was pregnant. She's drinking champagne, people!

So Julie lifts her glass and says, "dad, you do the toast for mom."

Larry looks like a deer caught in the headlights. He says, "What are we celebrating?"

We all stare at him as if he turned a putrid shade of green. "dad, mom retired today."

"She did?" He gives me the look.

I say, with all the authority of a recently retired schoolteacher, "Really, we've been discussing this for months, and now you claim ignorance?"

"I didn't know today was the day."

"Hint, the full glasses of champagne?"

"I thought we were celebrating Nic's new kitchen?"

"Dad, that was so last week."

In the meantime, we are all standing there holding our bubbly, with worried expressions clouding our recently cheerful faces. A wise person, I think it was Susan Newman, once wrote that the way you leave something is the way you enter what's next.

He looks around, lifts his glass, and says, "to mom's retirement."

"Now that's the way to wrap up a decade of work?"

"So, what's next?"

"My retirement plan is to get thrown in a minimum-security prison in Hawaii."

"I'll drive the getaway car."

Honestly, I'm no longer equipped to function in polite society. I don't remember how to wear makeup, real clothes, or shoes. This is the result of working from a lounge chair, in pajama bottoms, on Zoom for a year! Now, when people ask what I do for a living, I can say I'm a writer, and that will explain everything.

I've come to the end of a long road, but, as you know, when we think we've come to the end of the runway, that is when we learn to fly.

TOUGH TIMES DON'T LAST. TOUGH PEOPLE DO...

"Love and loathing can hold no surprises for most people in middle age. What we haven't gorged on, we've sampled."
–Robert Hillman

This is my husband's go-to phrase when I complain about the trials and tribulations of life, especially when I was outnumbered by children, Larry was traveling nonstop, and my mom lived two states away. It got to a point where he'd abridge the statement to, "Tough times don't last..."

You can only imagine my understated response. Yeah, it was primitive, unladylike, and unrepeatable. So don't ask.

I remember calling him to lament when the family minivan broke down once again. It was a brown and tan Ford Aerostar, and it could not have been uglier. We called her Reese after the peanut butter cups. She came with three rows of seats and opposing slider doors. The good thing about sliders is the doors don't get dinged when the kids pile out, but the bad thing is they get left open, which periodically drains the battery.

I could totally relate because much of the time, I felt drained.

So, one day, when my battery, I mean the car's battery, was completely dead, and I still had to chauffeur the kids to and from swim, soccer, basketball, etc., and my generous neighbor Bob was not home to lend me his car. I rang up Larry in desperation, who was vacationing, escaping, excuse me, working in Connecticut (could he be further away), and explained my woeful predicament.

His compassionate response, "Sounds like you're hosed."

"I'm hosed, am I?"

After I had t-shirts made up for me and all the kids that said, "I'm Hosed?" in bold letters across the front, I rented a deluxe Hummer for the rest of the week.

Yeah, I'll tell you who's hosed.

Anyhoo, so recently, I've been hearing the tired adage, "Tough times don't last…" and I'm not talking about reconstruction woes. Something much worse has transpired, and with no viable options, Larry has reverted to this impoverished euphemism.

If you don't want the full and unabridged edition, skip to the end because I plan on chronicling the series of unfortunate events in gruesome detail. Trigger warning: it's a dreadful tale, and you might develop empathy pains, high blood pressure, and an addiction to wine. Read at your own risk.

I'll paint you a picture as vivid as possible, so you'll barely have to use your imagination.

It's our last day up at the lake. The guests have all gone home. The laundry is done. The kitchen is cleaned. The bathrooms are spit-shined, and my Robo-vacuum is on the move. With the temperature hovering around a hundred degrees, and the humidity just over fifty percent, we decide conditions are excellent for an impromptu boat ride.

Fortunately, or not, we are still able to get our boat out of the lift and into the water. The lake is so low this year that by mid-July, we'll run out of cable and be forced to launch and recover the boat each time we want to use it. That's a total hassle, but you can't be stranded without a boat in the middle of summer.

No. No. No.

Larry heads down to the dock and engages in a rather prolonged battle with an army of gregarious spiders. They hang out under the dock in bulk, so when you lower it to get the boat in the water, the spiders climb onto the dock and into the boat as if an undeterrable rebel force. Keep in mind Larry is not really a spider guy.

I see him out in the middle of the lake with an armory of wet rags, trying diligently to knock the spiders off the boat. The problem is the spiders cleverly throw a web from the water and simply crawl back into the boat, but literally, there are hundreds of spiders and one towel raging defender. Let me just say it's not going well. It appears the spiders have the upper leg, so to speak. Larry's new strategy is to push as many spiders as possible into the water, then move the boat to another location, and repeat. It's way funnier watching than I'm able to describe, but my sense of humor is a little warped these days.

All worn out but victorious, he finally returns to the dock.

My stomach hurts from laughing so hard but Jim, Sue, Larry, and I manage to load up the boat with coolers, towels, and flotation devices, heading out to Buckingham to float in the cool water, sip a little wine, and shoot the shit.

It's as if we have not a care in the world, but this is about to change for one of us.

The water is extraordinarily refreshing, especially in this humid, hot weather. As time passes, we decide we need to check out Konocti Harbor and Resort, which recently opened for guests. Apparently, there is live music and cocktails tonight.

After scrambling into our wrinkled cover-ups and doing what we can with our wet hair, we head over to the new lakeside bar for a lookie-loo. By the grace of the lake God, we score a table and enjoy a refreshing cocktail with the smooth sounds of an acoustic guitarist.

When the music becomes too much for our aging ears, we decide to boat over to Lakeport for Pogo's Pizza, the perfect ending to a perfect evening. Yeah, not so fast, my friend.

The lake is eerily quiet. The water is ours and ours alone. Clear Lake is one of the richest lakes in the state when it comes to nutrients. That is one reason we have algae blooms and massive amounts of aquatic weeds. Some of these weeds have been in the lake for more than a million years. Can you imagine?

The most common weed is hydrilla. It's classified as an invasive weed, and this year, with the depth of the lake so low, the weeds are out of control. We made it halfway across the lake before the boat started overheating, and Larry had to get in the water in order to unravel the weeds from the prop. After tying up to the Lakeport dock, we ordered a large combo pizza.

Thirty-five minutes later, as the sun is setting in the western sky, we're enjoying the cool evening shade and a piping hot Pogo's pizza. This is the best pizza I've ever eaten. It's all about the crust, and the four of us dust off a large combo in record time.

After we've had our fill, we head back to Kono Tayee to enjoy the fire pit and a nightcap together.

Best laid plans...

We're all lulled by the smooth ride home. I'm sitting in the back-facing seat across from Larry, with Jim and Sue leaning against the seats along the stern of the boat. As Larry makes a sweeping turn just inside the buoy, he guns it (without warning), and as luck would have it, an unexpected wave meets the bow of the boat, and suddenly we're airborne, along with everyone in the boat.

I fly a foot into the air. That's saying a lot. I'm not exactly as light as a feather. Sadly, what goes up must come down, and I slam rib first into Larry's knee. The rest of me lands in a heap on the floor of the boat. There is a rather loud crack and horrendous moan as the wind is knocked out of me. I can't move or breathe or speak for several minutes. Not funny!

Jim says, "Are you okay?"

I shake my head no because I can't speak.

Sue says, "I heard the crack."

Larry says, "You hit my leg. You're fine."

When I regain my ability to verbalize, I scream, "What the hell, Larry?!"

The searing pain is nearly unbearable, and I'm not a wimp. I gave birth to four children without pain meds. But this? This is cruel and unusual punishment for the crime of a pleasant voyage. I struggle to stand when my ability to breathe returns.

Hobbling up to the house, I land in a deck chair and remain there for the rest of the evening. As the skies darken, so does my injury, and by bedtime, I can barely walk. Sneezing and coughing are out of the question.

I spent the entire night moving from couch to recliner and back to the bed. I couldn't get comfortable, and by morning, I was literally crying, "I can't sleep. My ribs hurt. Something is broken."

Poor Larry was trying to close-up the house, pack the car, and deal with his injured wife. He kept saying, "You'll be fine. It's just a nasty bruise."

With me walking around braless, aimlessly moaning, "I'm dying. I'm dying. Tell the kids I love them."

The ride home was not only exhausting but unpleasant for all concerned. I had to hold the seat belt away from my rib and elevate my braless boob so it wouldn't bounce on the wound. Try not to picture this in detail. I was a throbbing piece of agonizing flesh, and I did not hide my displeasure well.

When we arrived home, I could not find a comfortable position, and apparently, I was a little demanding.

We had a family dinner planned for tonight, so I sent Larry to the store with a lengthy list after he spent four hours putting together his new Napoleon barbecue. My daughters provided the salad and side dishes. Nic grilled while I directed the clean-up from my chair. I do what I can.

I'm finding out that I'm quite good at delegating, who knew, and I think it's going to be this way for quite some time. There's something beguiling about cracking a rib or two. You end up finding yourself in the broken bits because what I was doing and where I was going no longer exist. It allows you the time to finally just be without judgment or guilt. A new type of being is born, one who is more fearless than ever, one who fully understands, tough times don't last. Tough people do…

I'M SITTING IN HER PLACE

"It began in mystery and it will end in mystery, but what a rare and beautiful country lies in between."
–Diane Ackerman

This morning, I am sitting in my mother's place. It's early morning at the lake. The weather is as off as my mood, foggy, cool, placid. There is movement on the water, always moving, flowing north. Early morning is the best time at the lake. It is quiet and peaceful. Sleep still has me in its grasp, but the day is gently pulling me away. My thoughts last night, this morning, and tomorrow are focused on mom. I wish she were here, sitting in her spot at the end of the long green couch, the part of the couch that forms a lounge chair, feet up, covered with a brown furry blanket, gazing at the lake, sipping warm coffee, just as I am now.

"You want to come up to the lake?" This is the one question I always got a "yes" to from mom, even when we had fallen to the ground in the pouring rain and hit rock bottom. She loves being up here as much as I do, and this does not surprise me because so much of who I am is wrapped up in her. When I was young, I fought against our similarities. The last thing I wanted to be was my mother. Now, it is all I want.

I want to know who she thinks will win the bachelor next season. I want to watch her play Safeway monopoly, exclaiming over a free donut. I want to share coupons, exchange recipes, walk to the clubhouse, and sit in the sun. I want to know how she got the stains out of the carpet and the wilted orchid to survive. I want to enjoy a glass of wine with her after five, with ice and only one. That was her rule. I want to go bra shopping for my birthday. I want to know what she's reading. I want to grab a bite at *The Outback*. I want to have her as she had me, and I want her sitting in her place.

I want her laughing at my stories. I want to see her silly comments on my blog. I want to know what to plant in the full sun and under the shade of the arbor. I want someone who remembers me at five, sixteen, thirty-one, forty-nine, and fifty-seven. I want the woman who loves my imperfections and knows how to vanish my fears. I want to talk with her about my dad because she loved him the most. I want her to help me organize my hall closet and pick out new bath towels. I want her to watch my grandchildren grow. I want her to ask me about my day, my students, and my lesson plans. I want her memories, her love, her seasons.

I remember our last Mother's Day as if it was yesterday. I knew it would be just a matter of time before cancer claimed her, and I celebrated every day thereafter as if it were our last. She was sick for a long time, bravely fighting cancer that had taken ownership of her lungs. Taking care of her during this time was a gift, but one that came with many obligations and frustrations. I would see her often during those tough years. Her spirit was always there, but the woman who raised me was missing. She became soft, small, and quiet. She was doing the work of the dying. This is as laborious as birth, just as important, just as painful.

Helen Keller says, "Death is no more than passing from one room into another. But there's a difference for me, you know. Because in that other room, I shall be able to see." I think this is true for all of us, or at least I hope so. Sometimes death comes out of nowhere, and there is no time to process, appreciate, or prepare.

What we leave behind is the way we make people feel. It's what allows them to live authentically because we either honor each other's journey or stand in each other's way. This is really all we have to offer, and I'm forever grateful I had a mom who stayed the course, showed up, and chose love.

I remember when one of my children came down with a strange illness, one the doctors could not diagnose. Being a mother of four children, I knew this was serious. I would lie next to him for hours, offering water because he was too weak to hold the glass. Living in fear that I would lose him, I memorized every aspect of his face. The shape of his lips, the shape of his nose, the thick eyelashes, I counted the freckles on his nose. The perfect ears, the soft blond hair, and the brow line were all noted. I kissed his pink cheeks repeatedly. He survived, and the memory of him at five is etched in my brain forever.

I remember doing this with my dad, but that backfired a bit because I couldn't move past the last embrace, the last time we made eye contact, the last kiss goodbye. My lovely therapist/best friend Christine warned me not to stay in the last moments, to move back to the memories, the gifts that we get to keep.

When I was nearing the end of my time with mom, I memorized her face, the arthritic hands marked with age spots, the farmer's legs I massaged with lotion, but mostly the moments when she smiled. Her real gifts are so connected to who I am, and I'll carry those with me into this wild, wonderful life. The love of libraries and reading, antique stores and strolling, soup and egg sandwiches, dogs and cats, planting flowers in the spring. I'm sitting in her place literally and figuratively because that is what I have of her, the past, present and future she gifted me as my mother.

PART V: RECREATIONAL

THE LARRY FACTOR

"My whole body groans."
–Michael Kleber-Diggs

I wake up. Memories flood in, the time, the day, the season, the pandemic, the spike, the roommates, and praise be to God, the smell of coffee. At least I can smell. I tenderly stretch my aching body, yawn, blow my nose, and stare out the window with the only part of my anatomy that doesn't hurt. It's the same view from days, years, decades ago, and I never tire of it.

The view from my room is the back patio. This is the most beloved space on the property where memories of family and friends are so intertwined with the landscape, they've become inseparable.

Holding a warm cup of coffee in my hand, I allow the warmth from the cup to seep into my heavily treaded veins.

I have survived yet another day.

Can I just say Larry does not enter a room? He invades the once tranquil space as if a storm on the horizon (not to overuse an idiom), turning on the television, pushing back the drapes, and switching on lights. If he didn't bring me coffee, I'd bar his entry.

Larry slips into the wingback chair and says, "How you feeling this morning?" I believe that was followed by an inhuman smirk.

Very juvenile, in my opinion.

I pause before answering, gathering my composure, and say, "Like I've been beaten with a baseball bat repeatedly."

"I remember that all too well."

"Thanks for the warning, pal."

"Live and learn. That's my motto."

"I will remember that little piece of advice when you want to wax something. I stand on the adage, 'Do unto others what you would have them do unto you.' I believe it's attributed to Jesus?"

Was it only yesterday, because it feels like another lifetime, when Larry and I found ourselves all alone? I admit it was a little eerie, as if the rapture had occurred, and we were left behind.

Dante was working out of town for a few days. Julie, Nic, and the grandkids were celebrating Thanksgiving with Nic's family. Tony and Thalita were spending the evening with Adam and Kiana, and for a few brief hours, we became empty-nesters once again.

How much trouble could two people get into with only a few hours to kill?

You had to ask.

Here's the most reliable version of what went down. Okay, it's the only available account, and its fallibility is not up for debate.

Larry blasts into our room around 5:00 p.m., all excited and animated. He hands me a glass of wine and says, "Put Nora Ephron and her wrinkled neck back in the bookcase because I booked us some massages, and we're leaving in less than an hour."

He does this sort of thing now and then, claiming to know my innermost desires, and trust me, more often than not, he doesn't have a clue.

I say, "What? I want to go out to dinner, not have someone massage my generous flesh, and besides, I just did my hair." Giving my head a little shake for emphasis.

"Nice, we'll go out to eat after. You'll be all relaxed, then we'll come home and *rest* (code for anything but rest)."

"Honey, I really don't want to get naked, let some stranger slather oil all over my body, and then go out to dinner. The CDC would not approve."

"I already paid for it. I went over and checked it all out. It's a clean establishment, totally legit, and they are struggling for business. Have a heart."

"Really, now I'm responsible for the viability of massage parlors? It's not enough I'm single-handedly keeping Amazon in business."

"You mentioned you had a stiff neck. I'm just trying to be helpful."

I have no words.

This is why Larry is in sales. He does not take no for an answer. The next thing I know, I'm lying face down, naked between warm sheets, waiting for my masseuse.

Let me explain my trepidation. This is a Thai massage parlor. I've never had a Thai massage, and oddly enough, Larry was mum on the subject. While we were filling out our paperwork, he mentioned he wanted the Swedish massage (I'm Swedish. I could have done that for free, just sayin'), but it was a Thai place, so I thought it was rude to ask for a massage style from another country?

"I'll have the Thai massage," I emphasize, "thank you."

I'm escorted to a dimly lit room, but try to ignore the suspicious bars attached to the ceiling, and the red velvet wallpaper. Naturally, the only thought that occurs to me is, *dear God, run for your life!* But I was taught to be polite in all situations and running from the room screaming like a banshee could be considered ill-mannered.

I am anything but relaxed as I remove my clothes, fold them neatly on the chair, silently cursing my husband before slipping between the sheets.

A masseuse enters the room. She's soft-spoken. In fact, I could hardly understand her. Did she just ask if she could walk on my back? No, I must have heard that wrong.

She adjusts the sheets, slathers me with warm oil, and, for a minute, I believe I'm in heaven. Her touch is gentle, starting at my shoulders, working the slick oils into my neck and scalp. I'm going to have guido hair at dinner, but I no longer care. It feels so good.

Somewhere between heaven and hell, I hear a peculiar noise, as if someone is climbing on the furniture? Then I feel her bare feet descend on my spacious calves, not particularly comfortable, as she inches her way up my generous thighs, digging her vindictive toes into my unsuspecting muscle (It's both painful and disturbing). Slowly, with excruciating precision, she works her way over my voluptuous ass and onto my back. It's as if my body has become the Pacific Coast Trail. I'm finding it hard to breathe.

She follows these shenanigans with a new trick, worse than blazing trails along my spine. I hear her knuckles crack as she gets into position before jamming her elbow so deeply into my shoulder muscle, I could feel the skin on the other side of my body protrude. I lasted thirty seconds before screaming for mercy.

I'd have given up national secrets if I had any. As it was, I spewed the password to my iPhone and code for the keyless entry to the backdoor. It was incoherent rambling, but still.

This went on for an entire hour with the added bonus of her twisting my naked soma into a pretzel and then using her body weight to extend the pose. I'm just glad there are no cameras in the room. My trembling thigh, perfectly aligned with my ear couldn't have been a pretty sight.

Emily Weiss says, "I like a semi-stressful massage—one where I can really feel something being worked out." Well, let me just say I have been pulverized. The tension has been beaten out of me. I'm a human frappe.

I hear Larry's voice waffling up from the lobby. They must be done torturing him. His voice sounds lighthearted. Did I hear him laughing?

My ~~masochist~~ masseuse does a final deep tissue manipulation. She says, "Thank you," and quietly leaves the room. I freeze. Is she really gone? My next thought: is there a lock on the door?

Testing the probability for self-propelled motion, I try to wiggle my toes without moaning while calculating how much assistance I will need to get out of this damn bed.

I push through the pain, roll over, and gingerly sit up without fainting. Baby steps. Sliding my clean clothes over my oily limbs, I attempt to assemble my hair, which only makes it worse.

Opening the door slowly, I peek up and down the empty hall as if I'm trying to escape from Alcatraz. Ms. Light as a Feather is nowhere in sight.

I tiptoe to the lobby, where Larry is relaxing on the couch. He says, all sweet and relaxed, "Ready to go, honey?" His eyebrows lift ever so slightly as he takes in my burlesque-style hair but wisely keeps his thoughts to himself.

I couldn't get out of there fast enough.

Holding the door open so I can limp through, he says, "I paid your masseuse her tip, so that's all taken care of," as if I was worried about rewarding such brutality. Did you know the Latin word for tortura is *to twist*? Neither did I.

I remain silent. Did he just pay someone to literally walk all over me? There must be a message embedded in this situation, but I'm in too much pain to retrieve it.

How do these things keep happening to me? There must be a common denominator. Are you thinking what I'm thinking? Exactly.

We'll call it *the Larry factor*.

When we get in the car, I look over at Mr. Relaxed and say, "That was the most painful experience of my life, worse than four natural childbirths, all put together. What the hell?"

He says, "Yeah, that's why I went with the Swedish massage. I had a Thai massage once. I was sore for days. That lady wanted me to cry uncle, but I refused. She destroyed me. It was a battle of wills, and I won."

"Did you now? A covert warning would have been nice, something subtle, like wildly slashing your hand across your neck when I said, 'I'll have the Thai massage.' She pummeled and contorted my entire body for the better part of an hour, honey. I might need therapy?"

"Where should we go to dinner?"

"Somewhere with an expensive wine list."

"Split a burger at Willard Hicks?"

"Sure."

"Then we can go home and *rest*."

"Lord have mercy."

COLONS BEFORE COFFEE

"It's only awkward if it matters."
–Joyce Rachelle

There are some conversations that should never be discussed in the light of day. It's true. They should be confined to the pages of a nondescript journal, sequestered to the back of a dusty bookcase, maybe to be discovered postmortem. Life is not always graceful, and unfortunately for you, I process my experiences online, impulsively publishing my unfiltered thoughts with little regard for your sensitivities.

This is how the unpleasantness got out in the first place. All I can say is there is some reprehensible use of language, and you might consider this a courtesy warning.

"It's going to be a shit show," I think I hear Larry spew something of this manure as he enters our room, totally shattering my pristine dreamscape.

Now, just so you get the full picture, the sun hasn't fully risen. I'm still trying to make sense of my hazy world. In a complete fog, I struggle to remember where I am. Oddly enough, the curtains at the lake are taupe, and the ones at home are blue. I deduce we're home but squint at the man standing in the doorway to confirm it's my husband attempting to discuss colons before coffee.

Who does that?

Stretching my groggy limbs, I mumble something nondescript, "Things are called shit for a reason, dear."

He walks over, places a cup of coffee on my nightstand and a kiss on my lips.

I watch him settle into his recliner before he blatantly over shares, "I'm thinking of scheduling my colonoscopy for next week."

Attempting to adjust the pillows behind me, I offer a pleasant warning, "No bathroom talk before my first cup, please. Emily Post would be appalled."

Disregarding the established decorum, he says, "When are you due for your next one?"

After a proper glare, I say, "I'm enormously aghast to confirm there will be a sequel to Cheryl's Rectum. I got my notice a few weeks ago, which I'm planning to ignore for the time being. We're in the middle of a pandemic. It would be irresponsible."

"Let's schedule them together."

Is there anything more ghastly than picturing that sort of procedure with your husband holding your hand? I have no words, so I remain silent.

"Think about it. We'll have our Dulcolax cocktails before a liquid dinner. You can light some of those smelly candles, each of us traipsing off to our own restroom, clean as a whistle by morning."

"Yes, if memory serves, you scheduled your last one the day after Mother's Day?"

"I had to watch you slicing up your filet mignon while I sipped gallons of vile Kool-Aid."

"It was not the romantic evening I was envisioning. I believe you were quite testy about the prep?"

"A couple's cleanse. It'll bring our relationship to a whole new level."

The idea is ludicrous. I mimic his earlier claim. "It will definitely be a shit show."

Rubbing his chin, as if seriously considering this whole shindig, he says, "We'll have to stock up on ultra-soft toilet paper."

I laugh, claiming, "Bahaha, because you're full of crap."

He smiles and says, "I believe it's one of the few times in my life when I will not be full of shit!"

I lift my cup and offer, "To duo defecations. Honey, I need a refill."

As he gets up to grab my cup, he says, "We'll have to Uber."

"That will be interesting. Instead of drunk college students, they'll have to manage two elderly people, still high on Demerol, carrying their donut pillows."

"I'll treat you to a McDonald's breakfast biscuit after they're done filming our sequels."

"Honey, Netflix has nothing on us."

We moved on to more mundane topics, but the truth is, I believe words are strong enough to overcome what we fear, don't you? As Anne Morrow Lindbergh says, "Good communication is as stimulating as black coffee" and just as pungent in some cases.

All joking aside, a colonoscopy is the best screening test available for colorectal cancer, a lifesaving procedure, and a necessity for everyone at some point in life. It is the only screening test that also prevents many colorectal cancers, but unlike the COVID vaccine, people aren't lining up for their debut.

During a colonoscopy, your doctor examines the lining of your entire colon to check for polyps or tumors. These are the terminators of life. We want to know about them, so they can be removed immediately. It might sound uncomfortable and embarrassing, but there are many reasons we all need to schedule an appointment.

Unbeknownst to many, colon cancer is super common. It can run in families or happen randomly, but the best news is the procedure is simple and noninvasive. I agree. It's awkward as hell (so are mammograms). Maybe that's why the whole couple's colonoscopy has not taken off.

No excuses, you have the script, and as Milena Veen says, you too can be "... an inexhaustible source of awkwardness."

MUST LOVE DOGS

"When you are sorrowful look again in your heart, and you shall see that in truth you are weeping for that which has been your delight."
–Kahlil Gibran.

I wasn't going to belabor the death of my dog in yet another emotional essay.

I really wasn't.

But some strange force, not the least bit concerned about over analyzing personal tragedy in a public forum, took over, and I didn't have the strength to fight it.

The thing is you don't have to publish everything you write. Bahaha.

While that little thought is bouncing around in my head, my fingers are pounding out a sappy vignette on dealing with death.

Two words: it sucks.

I found out this week that grief pools with all the other grief that came before it, creating this cesspool of emotion that spills over one's entire being as if a vernal waterfall.

That's just my opinion, although I'm not sure I enjoy being referred to as a cesspool of emotion. It is what it is.

The bond we have with our dogs is unique, but to those who don't understand the emotional fallout after losing a beloved pet, this whole "I can't get a grip on myself" might seem odd.

Admittedly, I've been letting my emotions flow without delineation, much to the annoyance of my roommates, but hell, the last thing you want is to dam up your fervor because you're just putting off the inevitable burst at the first sign of a crack.

If I were a therapist, I'd say, in my professional opinion, I'm doing splendidly, considering I lost my shadow, and we all know Shaggy took it with him.

I have done all things distracting so as not to get hijacked by my unruly emotions.

I'll admit. The plan has holes.

I recruited Dante, who helped me put up the Christmas tree, and yes, I realize it is before Thanksgiving, but it required rearranging half the house for several hours, and this occupied my thoughts quite nicely.

I agree it goes against all the rules of holiday decorum, as if wearing white after Labor Day, and I don't care. In fact, the whole impropriety of it all makes me happy. I've become unscrupulous.

We've watched more Christmas movies than I care to admit. I've putzed around the house for no other reason than to revisit every place Shaggy has ever rested and I made several bad food and beverage choices.

Repeatedly.

But then I ordered a Portuguese water dog Christmas ornament, a Portuguese water dog wine stopper, and a Portuguese water dog doorstop, and honestly, I feel much better. I resisted the t-shirt and matching socks. Discipline at its finest.

Larry's completely baffled.

He says, "Every time you open wine, the front door, or look at the Christmas tree, you're going to be reminded of Shaggy?"

Me, "Yes, that's the general idea."

"Why?"

"I like being sad."

"Why don't you look at our visa? Now that's dismal."

"I'm going for heartbroken, not morose."

"I'm just trying to help."

"Are you now?"

On a more upbeat note, Larry and I celebrated thirty-eight years of marriage (twenty-five of which we've owned dogs, cats, or both, just sayin') the day after Shaggy died.

Thank God we were home when Shaggy's heart stopped beating, and someone wasn't watching him for us. Dante, Larry, and I were right there. Shaggy spent the entire day by my side and passed away minutes after Larry returned from the office. I believe he waited so Larry could say his final goodbye.

For our anniversary, Larry booked a room at the *Carmel Mission Ranch* and made reservations for dinner at *La Bicyclette*. He couldn't have dreamed up a better distraction. The scenery, the food, the hiking, and although every damn person had a dog, it was strangely comforting.

La Bicyclette, where we enjoyed our anniversary dinner, is known for its oysters and gnocchi, which we indulged in without remorse, soaking up the juices and sauces with warm French Bread. I know. I know. Totally bombed the diet, but it's my anniversary, and my dog died.

The minute I walk in the door of our home, I'm in trouble. Shaggy's presence is everywhere and nowhere.

There's not a place where his memory does not linger.

I keep checking to see if his water bowl is full, if he's curled up next to my chair, if he's ready for his evening scoop.

I visited with my sister one morning, and we had an absolute cry fest. We scheduled another one for next week if anyone cares to join us.

I discovered that it's best to be with people who love dogs when you let it leak out because they totally get it, and chances are they'll cry with you!

It's a thing.

All the Christmas presents for my grandkids are wrapped and under the tree.

I even cleaned out the refrigerator, which I despise.

Today, we (Larry) decided we were all going to clean out the garage. I'm not sure you fully understand the scope and sequence of this sort of project. See, I keep the house. Larry keeps the garage. Enough said.

Okay, I should add, the garage is a disaster of epic proportions.

Dante and I walk out there, fidgeting with our restless hands for a few minutes because there's no place to start, no end to the debris field, and a sense of doom is looming large.

Larry's in the driveway barking orders, which everyone is ignoring.

Dante and I load the goodwill stuff in my car, the trash in Larry's truck, and just when I think we've made some progress, Larry walks in and says, "What am I supposed to do with all that trash in my truck? What are we doing with this couch? There's no place for all these bikes (he has five). I've never seen these golf clubs in my life?"

I'm like, "Put the clubs in the side yard and maybe sack your attitude."

"Oh, you want to come with me and see the side yard? It's a disaster (he also keeps the side yards)."

I walk with him to check it out. There's like a couple of things stacked in front of his cupboard. I throw them all in the back of his truck. "There, all clear."

He opens his cupboard, and there are two additional sets of golf clubs in there covered with cobwebs. He says, "Where in the hell did these come from?"

"The golf fairy, geese. Put them in the goodwill pile if you don't want them."

Dante and I continue to sift through the rubble in the garage. Bins of ski gear go to the goodwill. Memory boxes for four kids get stacked under the window. Halloween costumes from when my kids were young go in the trash. Decorations for every known holiday get stored in the cupboards. Books, photo albums, decorations from a bridal shower we gave ten years ago... it's endless.

Larry, who has not moved a single item, says, "Why are you keeping all those baskets? Where is that wine refrigerator going to go? There won't be room for my car? We're wasting our time!"

Me, stomping my foot, hands-on-hips, "Could you just try to say one positive thing? We're busting our butts here, and all this grousing is counterproductive."

He stares at me as if I'm from another planet.

In my head, I'm printing up enough indulgences for an entire week.

Eventually, we've made ample space to put my exercise bike out there with an old television from my sister and still park his precious car. We've saved a chair and a couch. The rest is gone.

I'm dusty, exhausted, and haven't thought of Shaggy for hours.

Larry, who should have been tarred and feathered for his perfidy, says, "Would you like a glass of wine?"

And I finally realize this was Larry's plan all along… total distraction.

Dante and I collapse in the sitting room and wait for Larry to bring us our indulgences.

I'm dog-tired. I look around for my heart, who should be lounging beside me on the couch. His absence is woefully obvious.

I moan, "I miss Shaggy."

Dante and Larry collectively moan, "We know."

SPOILER ALERT

"We are surrounded by adversity but we shall triumph because we have a greater spirit."
–Lailah Gifty Akita

There is a chill in the marrow of my bones. I'm feeling my age today. The temperature outside has plummeted as I swallow back an acidity of fear pushing up from the core of my being.

I'm feeling dramatic, bear with me.

Cracking the flesh that confines my misgivings as if a walnut, I take the gnarled meat into my aging hand and consider how it resembles a brain.

The meat of fear is dense.

It does not matter if my basic fear is becoming invisible, invalid, or irrelevant, and yours is abandonment, loneliness, and ostracism. The truth is, our disquiet connects us, my fear pulling on yours, yours pulling on mine as if taffy until our toxicity becomes something new. A variant, if you will, more flexible than its original form and highly contagious.

Love does much the same.

My fears are not baseless (Ageism is real), but that does not make them valid, they are just fleeting thoughts that disrupt my inner sense of stability as if vertigo.

If you only knew the things I hold back, the frivolity I push down, the creativity I ignore because I think my words might offend, irritate, or annoy the hell out of someone.

I fear judgment more than cultivating my inner truth.

The problem is my words become as irrelevant as the evening news, especially if they're fake.

It's ridiculous that it takes an act of courage to wake up every morning and confront our current reality. No wonder I consume copious amounts of coffee and bacon.

It's as if we're drowning in a polarized pool of hatred that not only damages our quality of life, but our ability to feel joy. It's a poverty of spirit, and sadly, a reflection of our modern world. If it's not the wealth gap, climate change, or the pandemic, it's a conflict of power, privilege, and politics, which inevitably leads to an array of suffering, abuse, and addictions.

We live in dark times.

Screw the rashes. What I need is red wine, piquant cheese, and dark chocolate. In that order, plentiful, unlimited, and delivered by Door Dash.

We're all struggling, looking for a source of comfort and joy in the midst of a stark winter, staring out our window of reality, hoping for a personal advent to break through those musty curtains of indifference.

"Long lay the world in sin and error pining." I don't know about you, but I need my holy night, so my soul can feel it's worth.

What a mess. My lack of faith is showing, or maybe our collective apathy is attacking our faith in each other, in our dignity as a creation. "Faith includes noticing the mess, the emptiness, and discomfort, and letting it be there until some light returns," says Anne Lamott.

Maybe what I need is a change of scenery? While I'm envisioning luaus, Mai Tais, and stellar sunsets, Larry's listening to the weather.

As we hit the road, a mild storm chases us up the Interstate, but we arrive at the lake just before the skies open, and much-needed rain deluges us.

The good news is our DIY sealants held. There is no river of water trailing down the main window, dripping from the vent in our room, or flooding the lanai.

We quickly settle into our preferred spaces, me swaddled in the double-wide, writing with as much relevancy as possible from my little corner of the world. Larry is on the sofa opposite the television, excited to watch a taped version of the Formula 1 championship.

All day he avoided the news so as not to ruin the live experience.

It's interesting how we tend to eschew the outcome, the answer, and the conclusion before we've had a personal encounter.

I look up from my computer as he cranks up the volume on the television. He's off the couch in a single leap, making noises no grown man should make.

I'm like, "What the hell? Are you having appendicitis?"

Larry says, "It's the final lap of the race!"

"Thank God. I thought I was going to have to perform CPR."

I get the look.

Suddenly, he's jumping in the air, fists flying, yelling, "Oh My God, Verstappen is trying to pass Hamilton. Look at this. Look at this. He's doing it. Holy shit. Come on."

His excitement is contagious, and I rise from my berth to stand beside him.

A thrill of hope seizes our weary souls as Larry declares, "He did it! He overcame Hamilton! Unbelievable!"

You don't have to be male to enjoy competitions, rivalries, or sporting events. It's communal. We're drawn to it innately, and although it can be a source of conflict, we celebrate enmity in our culture.

It's much the same with ritual, worship, and faith traditions, but it's as if we've thrown out the baby with the bathwater, and now we're left with an emptiness that is difficult to fill.

We can enjoy Christmas without believing in the birth of Christ, many do, but remember, it's just materialism if you leave out the unwed mother, a woman who found herself unwelcome and alone, struggling to give birth to her first child, a child no one expected.

Life is a mystery. I don't know the future, and I prefer to keep it an enigma, but this much I know to be true…

Darkness is dangerously close to overtaking our world. No wonder we chose December, the winter solstice, to wait in joyful hope for the glorious light to redeem us. It's a close race. The outcome is unknown, but we can stand together, cheering on the underdog from Bethlehem until the bitter end.

Spoiler alert: Love wins.

STANDING ON THE PARKING LOT OF LIFE

"Sometimes we are so busy looking up and looking forward trying to figure out the next moves in our lives—or looking backward at all the places we have been — that we don't look down and figure out where we actually are."
–Bob Goff

The Return

As we pull into the parking lot of Larry's and my first apartment off SW Murry Boulevard in Beaverton, Oregon, 38 years melt away, and suddenly, we're 23, newlyweds, standing in the parking lot of our new home with our entire life ahead of us, but we have no idea how this joint venture will engulf us, as if Jonah in the whale, only to be released nearly 40 years later, spit out where it all began.

You know me. I'm subjected by my own impulses as I wrestle with these polarized versions of myself, one wrinkled, one freshly pressed... both forged from the same fabric.

Ahead of us lay decades of good and bad decisions we've yet to make, children we've yet to create, friends we've yet to meet, abundant opportunities we've yet to encounter, and then there's *the thing we didn't know*.

In November 1983, we were returning from our honeymoon in Puerto Vallarta, Mexico. We landed in San Jose and drove to the Northwest with my in-laws as we were planning to gather in Chehalis, Washington, the next day to open our wedding gifts now stored at my parents' home.

After years of our parents trying to keep us out of the same bed, we're suddenly allowed to sleep together. That was sort of mind-blowing. We would spend our first night in our first home as a married couple with my in-laws in the next room, slumbering on a fold-out bed with mismatched sheets, Larry and I giggling into our pillows.

The good old days.

Stepping out of the car in 2022, I stare at the small apartment complex and try to remember which unit was ours.

Larry makes his way confidently up the sidewalk. I follow (story of my life), arriving at the very back of the building, gazing up a single flight of stairs, and the threshold to our new life comes into view. Apartment number 4808, images of passing through that portal assuage my mind, both casual and ceremonial, joyful and piqued, but always with the energy and enthusiasm of youth.

Everything is different, but nothing has changed, as if we have been incarnated into another womb.

After walking all over the dilapidated property and checking out the pool that froze solid in December of '83, we conclude the general condition of the building is well past its prime, not unlike ourselves.

Driving the streets of our little town, remembering the breakfast joints we frequented and the places we shopped for groceries, I can't help but acknowledge these memories are shrouded in a veil of innocence. It was the last weeks of 1983, as the wise men drew closer to the baby in the manger, we began our life as one, naively optimistic, unsullied as a newborn.

Forging ahead with very little life experience, money, or imagination, we made our fair share of *interesting decisions*, but as I've noted before, the best thing about the past is it's the past.

I admit I'm overly obsessed with the rearview mirror, if you will, but as you know, the images appear larger than the reality, and, for that reason alone, I believe the past should be properly disposed of, don't you?

The Burial

Let's consider it a moral act of bravery, an act that not only releases us from the umbilical cord of yesterday but entombs those decisions in the past because clearly if those corpses never receive a proper burial, no words spoken on their behalf, no prayers offered for their eternal rest, they'll haunt you. Seriously.

I could have been…

I should have done…

What the hell was I thinking?

The thing is, like many of us, my world has always been envisioned with a heavy Judaio–Christian influence. You know what I mean? It's how I made sense of things. This philosophy claims there are no arbitrary events. Everything that happens is part of a plan. It happens for a reason, and that alone belongs to God. Susan Sontag puts it this way, "… every crucifixion must be topped by a resurrection. Every disaster or calamity must be seen either as leading to a greater good or else as just and adequate punishment fully merited by the sufferer." Damn, that girl was brilliant.

But honestly, I've come to believe this is a rather restrictive, naïve, parochial view of our glorious but imperfect world. Is it wrong? I don't know. I question the validity that every hardship is intrinsic to the "greater good" in a free-range world because, unlike chickens, I think we build our own cages.

Decisions are consequential by nature, some more than others. Even the most insignificant ones can be far-reaching. I'm not smart enough to delineate the purpose and meaning of life, but at my age, you see patterns. Patterns in our decision-making, patterns in the consequences of our decisions, patterns in our communication, and it doesn't matter whether we're deciding on dinner options, a new sofa, or the outcome of an argument, there's a pattern to our thinking, an equation if you will, and can I just say? I'm always right. Bahaha.

I've noticed how suffering is derived from selfish decisions, but pleasure is different. It springs from a genuine giving of the self, as in marriage, sex, forgiveness, food preparation, and even charity, but more importantly, it seems to be the crux of all our relationships, including the relationship we have with ourselves.

Ironically, Larry and I are in Portland, Oregon, for the wedding of our dear friend's son Christopher to a lovely woman named Emily, and they will start their life in the rugged Northwest, just as we did. I consider that a good omen.

The Trip Down Memory Lane

We arrive a day early, so Larry and I can make a nostalgic trip to Chehalis, Washington, where my parents lived for over forty years, where parts of my father's ashes are scattered, and memories of my beloved mom and dad are so braided with the landscape I feel myself unplaiting with each mile.

Our children spent a lot of time in the Northwest. We made the trip several times a year to hang out at the family homestead on Donahoe Road. Eleven acres of heavily forested land on the edge of town, surrounded by fields of corn and peas, with a meandering creek, made it feel as if we were existing in a fairytale.

Driving all over town in our rental car, we check out dad's old factories, the kid's Penny Playground, the movie house, mom's church, the Elk's Club, downtown, the old hotel later made into apartments, the vintage library on the hill, even the Rib Eye Steak House with their famous peanut butter pie.

The present rarely matches up with the version we hold of the past. Even if the changes are subtle, they can be catastrophic to our treasured memories. Let me just say it wasn't the same. It was shockingly different, and I feel as if the levy between past and present has been forged.

The Present

Early the next morning, at the Residence Inn in downtown Portland, we slip into our sweats and walk the streets of Portland, trying to understand the destruction and carnage of this beautiful waterfront downtown. It's painful to witness the disfigurement of once-thriving cafes, storefronts, and offices. I understand the importance of protest, how change happens, and how the rights of the victim must be rectified, claimed, fought for, but the aftermath of destruction is disturbing, often cloaking the message in violence.

Maybe it is from these very ashes that change will ultimately arise. I don't know, but as my kids say, I'm old, biased and less malleable as I age, but alas, isn't that my inherent value?

I'm predictable.

The highlight of this weekend was all the time we were able to spend in the presence of old friends, as Jill said, "It's so rare we have an entire day together, makes me tear up remembering the laughter and joy on the faces of my dearest friends, gathered at the local sports bar, cheering on the 49ers."

The Ride

Speaking of poignant observations, our Uber ride to the wedding was rather bizarre and a little disconcerting. Steve and Jill order up a ride via their phone. We're running a tad late, and our anxiety is gathering momentum as if the beginning of the Grand Prix. The ride finally pulls up to the curb, and the four of us rush to infiltrate the economy-sized car. The first thing I notice is the upholstered seats are covered in bird shit. Then I hear an actual bird chirping as we hesitantly cram ourselves into the rancid interior.

The wedding starts in ten minutes, and our options are severely limited.

Larry squeezes into the front seat, knees practically in his chest, while Steve, Jill, and I are gingerly perched on the edge of the back seat, traumatized by the live bird actually sitting on the driver's head. Yes, that's not a typo. There is a lime green bird sitting on a pile of matted hair and chirping as if it had not a care in the world. Thank God it is only a three-minute ride, and we exit the car as quickly as possible. No tip!

Later that evening, as Larry is extrapolating about his extraordinary observation skills, we find ourselves in a deep discussion about the strangest Uber rider ever.

Steve says, "What about that bird?"

Larry says, "What bird?"

Jill, Steve, and I, in unison, say, "Seriously?"

"I didn't see any bird. I was just worried about all the bird shit and feed scattered all over the car."

I say, "There was a bird sitting on the driver's head, not twelve inches from your face?"

"I never saw it."

"FBI."

I get the look (patterns).

The Wedding

The wedding venue is gorgeous, a combination of charming brick archways, old beams with an appealing industrial feel, and stunning flower arrangements. We are greeted by an attentive staff who warmly invites us into the space, offering us refreshing adult beverages as we relax and enjoy the company of those gathered for this momentous but intimate event.

The ceremony is captivating, moving, and pivotal to the future Chris and Emily are envisioning. As the bride and groom bask in the glow of marital bliss, it seems as if their life is an oyster, just waiting to be opened! We spend the evening not only witnessing the vows of young love but listening to heartfelt speeches as family and friends lift their glasses to the newlyweds. Honored to be a part of their nuptial celebration, we sip excellent wine, break bread, and express our joy on the dance floor.

The Synopsis

But here's the thing they don't know, the thing that took me years to absorb, the thing I struggle to fully embrace…

Our choices matter. The past cannot be repurposed. What I do on a daily basis is indicative of what I value and what I deem worthy of my time. Opportunities are time sensitive. They appear randomly throughout our life as if a banquet and what we consume either nourishes us or depletes us.

Oh, how I abhorred cutting the cord to my childish ways, adopting a more magnanimous approach to life, but the one thing maturity has to offer, aside from the obvious, is a broader perspective, a bird's-eye view if you will. To interpret our history is maybe to impoverish it, a depletion of sorts, one that attempts to make us more comfortable with our choices. The truth is we're all standing in the parking lot of life, looking for the portal to our dreams, and crossing that threshold should always be ceremonial.

TRUST YOUR HUSBAND

"Life should not be a journey to the grave with the intention of arriving safely in a pretty and well-preserved body, but rather to skid in broadside in a cloud of smoke, thoroughly used up, totally worn out, and loudly proclaiming "Wow! What a Ride!"
–Hunter S. Thompson

The aftermath of Christmas is not unlike bringing a newborn home. There are the sleepless nights (overindulging on Netflix much), people in need of calming (as the bills come in), and for reasons unknown, the laundry room is full of wet towels, soiled garments, and linens embroidered with jolly St. Nick.

Am I the only one?

So, out of these domestic musings, Larry says early one morning, "Pack a bag, honey. We're going on a ride." And by ride, he means, as in the Flintstones, where my feet are what power the vehicle. In this case, we're talking about a tandem bike, the Christmas gift I somehow got roped into, the thing that has become our 2022 linchpin, along with padded biking pants (like my butt wasn't big enough), and riding gloves.

"Wait a minute. My weather app says a storm is coming in later today and tomorrow, and I'm not keen on riding in the rain."

"If we leave by 9:00 (mind you, it's currently 6:45 a.m.), I think we'll just make the window."

"The window?"

"Yes, as in, we'll ride in between the two storms."

"It's rather cold and windy, don't you think?" The truth is I'm snuggled in my warm bed, fire softly burning, contemplating my next post. I would prefer to remain in this state of utter bliss for the next several hours, after which I plan to exercise on my stationary bike (not in a storm) and maybe organize the fish bathroom or spruce up the kitchen. I know… gives me the shivers too.

Speaking of shivers, he says, "Yeah, you'll need gloves and a warm jacket."

Out of curiosity, I say, "What exactly am I packing for? And where are you (emphasis on you) planning on riding?" I think those are fair questions, given the circumstances.

"Half Moon Bay. I booked a room. The hotel is right across from the beach. Our balcony faces the ocean. The paved trail we want to catch runs right in front of the hotel. It'll be the perfect practice ride for our Palm Springs trip." (Larry signed us up for a 50-mile ride in the desert in February, which seemed miles away in 2021, but inches closer, as if a tarantula.)

Here I'm visualizing a warm fire, endless cups of coffee, and reading a few pages from the book Seth recommended. A novel so important it has the capacity to change the trajectory of the entire world, the one that came in the mail two weeks ago, and yet I'm still on page seven.

As G.K. Chesterton claims, "An adventure is only an inconvenience rightly considered. An inconvenience is only an adventure wrongly considered." Interesting, don't you think? Adventure and inconvenience appear in both statements. Like marriage, it's as if they're a pair.

I say, "So we're spending the night?"

He says, "Yes, and there's a great restaurant we can walk to for dinner."

"So, I'll need heels and a dress?"

"It's casual. You can wear your biking pants if you want."

"I'm not that kind of girl."

"Don't I know it? Hey, I'm going for a ride with Stu. Be ready to head out by the time I get back."

"You're going for a ride before our ride?"

"Yes, a warm-up."

"A refill before you go." I hold up my coffee mug.

When he returns with the hot cup of coffee, I lean back into my pillows and consider falling back asleep. I mean, he'll be gone at least an hour or two. It's not like I'm washing my hair just so I can stuff it into a bike helmet all day, all sweaty and windblown. If I've calculated it correctly, it'll take me five-minutes to shower, slip into my biking pants, throw on a couple of warm shirts, my ski coat, tennis shoes, and gloves. I can pack a pair of jeans and a sweater for dinner, a toothbrush, sunscreen, some earrings, and my adorable booties.

In my mind, I'm done, so I relax, knowing I could be ready in 15 minutes tops.

Relaxing back into my pillows, I grab my new book and return to my musings on page seven.

That's when I hear the door open. What the hell? Has it already been an hour? Shit! It's been over an hour. How time flies when you're relaxing for the first time all damn year? (Granted, it's only the 2nd of January, but still!)

Larry blasts into the room, bringing the cold air with him. He says, "Well, I can see you're ready to go."

"That was a fast ride?" I say as I scramble out of bed, knocking a pile of folded laundry off the hope chest.

"Not really. It's been over an hour, and by the way, we're leaving in fifteen minutes."

"Stop for coffees on the way out?"

"If you hurry."

When it comes to coffee, I can be quite motivated, showered, geared up, and packed in mere minutes. It may have seemed longer to Larry, but he's a type A. He doesn't understand time as I do. It's not an exact science. Time follows my schedule, not the other way around.

He had to take both the wheels off the bike to get it in the car. The contraption has a massive frame. We had to put our bags on top, helmets on the floor, while my boots got thrown under the wheels.

The purpose of life is to live it, to taste experience to the utmost, to reach out eagerly and without fear for newer and richer experiences, says Eleanor Roosevelt. There's wisdom in that statement. I just can't find it.

Arriving in Half Moon Bay, we're delighted to find our room at the Oceanfront Hotel is ready, and we don't have to leave our belongings in the car. The hotel is unique. The word funky comes to mind. Larry was right. It's located right along the coast, literally. The waves are crashing not twelve feet away from the entrance. Gigantic cement stilts elevate the entire building. If the tide washes up, it can just flow right through the building. Let's hope that doesn't happen tonight.

The structure is old and fairly dated, but I am charmed by all the trinkets and paraphernalia the owner, Ann, has decided to showcase. The lobby is full of surprises. A coffee bar is set up in the corner, all for free, and a snack area by the front desk fully stocked with fruits, beverages, wine, and nuts. There's an old dusty bookcase stuffed with classic novels from floor to ceiling, and on every available surface are nautical doohickeys that are somehow pleasing to the eye.

Our room, named the Carmel, is gorgeous, and I can't stop gloating over the fact the floors are heated. A beautifully dressed king-sized bed anchors the spacious room, and there is a small balcony overlooking the ocean with two large windows that let in soothing light. There is a cozy gas fireplace for even more ambiance. The jacuzzi tub in the bathroom looks brand new. It butts up against a glass shower, double sinks, and those heated floors. My toes are overjoyed. In the closet, two vintage robes hang on wooden hangers, one grey and one pink.

How adorable. Envisioning Larry in the pink one makes me smile.

I'm barely able to use the facilities when Larry is chasing me out the door, so we can put the bike together and get on with our ride. As you know we're timing our ride between storms which I find endlessly amusing as it mimics my life.

Putting the wheels back on the bike is not as easy as taking them off. It never is, but we manage with a fair amount of cussing, straining, and complaining. Before I could remark about the shockingly cool temperature, we were on the bike and making our way along the mesmerizing coast.

The trail is nicely paved; apparently everyone else had the same idea and maneuvering our huge monster bike past groups of walkers is tricky. I'm on the back, and can't see anything in front of me, as Larry's back blocks my view. I depend on him to verbally warn me about what's coming up, when I'm supposed to glide, when to lean into a sharp turn, etc.

Let's just say we're a work in progress.

The responses we get from the people we pass on the trail are hysterical. One couple felt the need to yell out, "We used to have one of those!"

Larry slows the bike to say, "Yeah, how did you like it?"

The wife says, "It didn't work out for us. I couldn't stand being on the back with no control. We sold the tandem. We're much better at riding our own bikes. At least we're still married."

The husband says, "This woman is particularly difficult. You'll be fine. Trust your husband."

I yell back, "He keeps telling me control is an illusion." I hear them laughing as we round the bend.

After about six or seven smooth miles, I find myself marveling over the beauty of the ocean, the charming houses docked along the path, the flora and fauna, and the sun warming my back. I'm silently overflowing with gratitude for the opportunity to experience such exquisite scenery when suddenly the topography changes, as in life. Things get turbid.

Just beyond the pine trees, the trail is no longer paved. In fact, we find ourselves riding on a bog. It's wet, extremely muddy, and difficult to maneuver this monstrosity. We're forced to get off the bike repeatedly and walk through the worst areas, or should I say Larry has to walk the bike through the muck. I tiptoe around leaping over the puddles as if a ballerina.

Larry looks rather bedraggled. He says, "This is not fun."

Every time we get back on the bike, we practically tank on the slippery ruts. I moan. "The mud is spattering off the back wheel. It looks as if I pooped my pants. I'm a human fender."

He laughs. "That happens when you're riding in the mud. We should get back on the paved trail. This is not working."

"See, we do agree on some things."

So, after walking most of the way back, we return to the paved trail and try to avoid mowing over the pedestrians milling about.

There is one tense moment when we come upon a group of eight or nine walkers. They're chatting it up, taking over the entire path. Larry yells several warnings, "On your left. On your LEFT! ON YOUR LEFT!" No response. They just keep sauntering along until we almost crash into a few of them as we attempt to come to a full stop. The bike is heavy, especially with the two of us riding. It's impossible to stop on a dime. If people don't move over to allow us to pass, it gets ugly.

Well, they have words. Larry has words while I try to pretend to be Switzerland and remain perfectly silent until I'm sure no one is going to throw a rock at my back.

Then I say in a loud, clear voice, "If I am going to be riding behind you, TRUSTING MY HUSBAND, I expect better behavior when it comes to the pedestrians."

"I know. I was out of line."

"Good, I think I need a Bloody Mary."

"Sam's Chowder House is about five miles up the road here. We'll stop there for lunch."

"Well earned, I'd say."

"It's been an interesting ride."

"That's one way to put it."

After lunch, we get back on the muddy bike and ride another ten miles before calling it a night. We complete about twenty-five miles total between storms, and I am ready for a warm shower, a warm meal, and a glass of wine.

As you can imagine, life has other plans.

After sprucing up, we come downstairs and linger by our car for a minute, trying to decide if we want to drive across town to the Mezza Luna Italian restaurant or just eat at the local joint, Miramar Beach restaurant, located right across the street. While we're standing there in the dark, this random lady walks up to our car, parked not ten feet from us, and starts looking in the car windows.

Now, if I were to describe her, I'd say she was shady looking with a creepy presence (I really should have gone into law enforcement).

Larry walks up behind her and says, "What the hell are you doing? Looking for something to steal?"

I'm desperately digging my phone out of my purse in case I need to call 911.

She moves around him, ignoring his question, and starts walking away.

Larry says, "I'm taking your photo, and I'm sending it to the police."

Not fazed in the least, she keeps walking and disappears into the night.

I'm like, "That's crazy."

Larry says, "She was casing the parking lot for cars to break into."

We decide to move our car closer to the hotel parking lot under a floodlight and eat across the street, so we can keep an eye on things. I can't imagine she wants a muddy tandem bike.

After a scrumptious dinner, we fall asleep listening to the sound of the surf crashing against the shore, enjoy a leisurely breakfast near the wharf early the next morning, and while driving home along the coast, we identify several other biking trails we might want to try someday.

I say as we pull into our driveway, "Now that was a great adventure."

He says, "I told you so."

I smile and say, "My knight in shining armor would never say I told you so."

"I'm not your knight. I'm the guy who brings you coffee in bed. I'm more like your houseboy."

"In that case, if you could bring in my boots and my bag."

I get the look, the one I've come to know, to love and trust.

BUILT TO LAST

———————————
————————

"The propensity to truck, barter and exchange one thing for another is common to all men, and to be found in no other race of animals."
–Adam Smith

I accuse Larry, with a saucy attitude. "You woke me up at 3:00 a.m. I tossed and turned the rest of the night."

"I remembered I had to transfer some money."

"At 3:00 a.m.?"

"Better late than never."

"And then you said you were going to wake me up at 6:00 a.m., and it's only 5:00 a.m."

"I'm excited."

"Hello, it's not Christmas."

"It's better."

"It's still dark."

"Let's get going."

God As My Witness

Here's the full Monty, the unabridged version, and fair warning, it's sordid as hell.

Larry's been hankering for a new truck for months. I mean, as soon as we got the tandem bike, the only thing I see on his computer screen, as I travel from kitchen to laundry room, is trucks! Yes, I have a Cinderella complex because *I can be whatever I want to be.*

The problem is when Larry wants something, Larry is going to get something, come hell or high water. If you pulled off his toenails one at a time, he would still say, this isn't true. This, my friend, is self-deception at its finest.

Moving on...

As you know, the value of used cars has skyrocketed recently, most likely due to the chip shortage leaving new cars stalled on production lines across America. Larry has calculated the net worth of two of his old cars, and with ADDITIONAL FUNDS, that's key, he can get the truck of his dreams.

Like I said in the beginning, if you need a truck, like a marriage, find one that's built to last.

I want to find sleep, nothing excessive, just two uninterrupted hours.

It just so happens the truck Larry wants is in Reno, as in Reno, Nevada, four hours away in the best of traffic, and might I mention the price of gas?

And he wants his sleep-deprived wife to drive because he needs to work. There might not be enough coffee in the world, but I'm going to find out.

A Snafu of Epic Proportions

Rolling down Highway 80, I have to say when we hit the snow line, there is honestly no prettier sight than the Sierras covered in snow. I'm charmed, but I need to go to the bathroom something fierce and it's distracting as hell.

Halfway there, we pull off the highway to fill up both the car and my coffee mug, but the bathroom is out of order, and there is no coffee. Are you kidding? I should have worn a diaper and brought a thermos. Larry's in a mild state of panic. He doesn't want to miss his appointment, have the damn truck of his dreams sold out from under him, and then we just drove 250 miles in the middle of the night for nothing.

For weeks, Larry has been quibbling with some sales guy over the price of a particular truck while simultaneously bartering over the price he wants for his trade-in. If you happened to miss last week's blog (no shame), I mentioned his decision not to sell his old truck to a local service that offered him more than this dealership in RENO, NEVADA, of all places.

Larry is a mystery of epic proportions. I'm sure he has his reasons, but they're not reasonable.

We arrive at the dealership right on time, 10:00 a.m. sharp, and I make a beeline for the lady's room. All I can say is the relief is real, except for the party in the next stall. She's not dealing with number one, if you get my drift. She must have eaten an entire cow last night. I exit quickly, holding my breath as I wash my hands. It's tricky.

In the meantime, a young man named Donovan (love that name) approaches Larry and asks if he can help. To give you a complete picture, Donovan is missing half of one arm. His coat sleeve is pushed halfway up, so the stump is visible. He's maybe in his early thirties, dressed in slacks and a dark blue jacket, sporting a baseball cap. Not sure that's a good sign?

Larry says, "I have an appointment with Dave at 10:00 a.m. to see a truck we've been discussing."

Donovan says, "Dave's not here (reminds me of that Cheech and Chong clip ~ hysterical).

"We have an appointment?" He's holding up the appointment reminder on his phone as if that has any bearing on our current reality.

Donovan smiles, holds out his one hand in resignation, and says, "Well, Dave's not here today. He must have thought Lance would be able to show you around. He's Dave's assistant, but unfortunately, Lance is off today, too. What truck did you want to see? I'd be happy to show you."

Larry runs a hand across his brow. He says, "It is a white, four-door, F150, platinum."

I want to add, "built to last," but I think better of it and remain silent.

"I know the one. It's not here either. Can I show you another one that is similar?"

Are you thinking what I'm thinking?

Holy Shit.

Larry's body language alone is enough to send half the sales guys scampering under their desks for cover.

As bad as that latrine was, I wish I'd stayed.

Larry laments loudly, coarsely, and precisely. As not to traumatize you, I'll leave the exact verbiage to your imagination. Finally, he says, "Cheryl, get in the car. We're going home."

You Can't Make This Shit Up

Poor Donovan, he's sweating, and it's only 30 degrees out. He says, "If you give me a few minutes, I'll find that truck and bring it back, but in the meantime, you can look at a similar version and check out the features. Does that work for you?"

If you want to rile my husband, all you need to do is show up late for an appointment. If you really want to piss him off, don't show up at all. If you want trouble with a capital T, hide the object of his desire and watch the axes of the world shift.

By the grace of God, Larry agrees, begrudgingly (meaning he is not his normal warm and fuzzy self). I'm giving him the look, which he totally ignores, and we follow Donny (as he likes to be called) across the lot to the like version. He leaves us with an open truck to explore the features while he tries to figure out where the hell the other truck is.

I'm sure Donny is ruing his decision to come to work today.

Larry is incredulous. He's talking to himself, muttering obscenities as if a drunken sailor. I'm sure my mother is up there blushing from a safe distance.

I choose to purposely silence every one of my predictable thoughts, as they are far too scorching and clearly will not aid the situation.

Long story short, our hero Donny somehow found the truck at the airport (five miles away). The general manager had caught a flight out this morning and left the truck in the long-term parking lot. I can't wait until Dave gets back in town and discovers his ride is missing.

Donny and another sales guy drove around the parking lot, pressing the fob until the truck sounded its horn.

Donny pulls into the parking lot, all out of breath, holding up the keys, and says, "Take her out for a test drive. Take all the time you need. I just need a copy of your license." I'm about to offer myself as collateral, but I can see Larry's humor has soured. It's as if I'm clairvoyant.

Larry takes a leisurely stroll around the truck, kicking the tires as he goes. When he finishes circling his prey, he takes the keys from Donny's one hand, hands him a license, and says, "I'll be back," Arnold Schwarzenegger style.

Drama much? Donny is praying the tank is full, and we stay out all day.

This truck is huge. There is a stair that pops out when you open the door, so you can climb into the cab as if scaling a jungle gym. It must be a guy thing? If they wore high heels and dresses, there would be a lift.

Larry drives around town gunning the engine, jumps on the freeway, and discovers this truck has some kick to it and a nice set of speakers. He's satisfied. This truck is a good fit and damn if it's not built to last. Don't get all emotional, it's just a metaphor.

By the time we pull back into the car lot, Larry's blood pressure has returned to normal, and he's ready to negotiate. I'm ready for a stiff drink and a couple of Xanax. It's everything he wants and more (I'll tell you about that later), and all we need to do is settle on a price.

I'd rather have a crown put in my back tooth, but that's just me.

Did I Remember Deodorant

We find ourselves seated in the front showroom. The dealership is crowded with buyers. Just about every desk has groups of nervous-looking clients and smiling sales guys, all wearing the same jacket. People are rushing back and forth from their desks to the offices with important-looking papers. As if a beehive, it's a swarm of activity, and I believe we're about to get stung.

Larry is the epitome of calm and calculating. I'm obsessed with their espresso machine. It's free, and the coffee is worthy. Currently, I've enjoyed two lattes and a mocha. I'm a little shaky, but fully functional.

Donny is typing our information into the computer, when Larry says, "Are you typing with both your hand and stump?" I'm not kidding. Mortified, I choke on my coffee and pretend there is something dire on my phone that needs my attention.

Is it hot in here?

Now Donny is one smooth cat. I'm sure he's used to these sorts of observations. He says, "I am. I've developed my own style, but it works."

Larry says, "It sure does."

While Donny continues to gather our information, asking about income, residence, and where we want to register the truck, Larry asks him how long he's been selling cars.

Donny says, "About three years. I've been doing quite well. I'm in between chemo treatments right now, so I work when I feel good and rest when I can't. The dealership has been good to me."

OMG, he has one arm and cancer!

Larry says, "Is that how you lost your arm? A Dravecky sort of thing?" I quickly look up Dravecky on my phone, and now all I want to do is slither out of the showroom and run to the nearest bar.

Donny looks up at Larry. He says, "No, not that way."

Larry says, "You know Dravecky? You might be too young."

Suddenly, I'm sweating profusely.

"I know of him." He holds up his stump and says, "I was born this way, bad luck twice, but I beat cancer, just finishing up the treatments."

My hand is aching to slap my husband silly.

"Well, I wish you luck."

"Thank you."

Hell No

There are brief back-and-forth negotiations. I'm impressed with the efficiency, but when Donny comes back with the final offer, it's not to Larry's liking, and you can probably guess what comes next.

Larry says, "No, this won't work. Sorry, but I can't leave that much money on the table, Donny. I'll take my car home, sell it myself, and check back on the truck next week. Come on, Cheryl. Let's go."

If you could send me a postcard with the following message in bold, so I don't forget. **I'm never, ever coming with Larry to buy a car again, not even if it's a convertible Jaguar, and he's buying it for me!** I might have it tattooed down the center of my arm.

I gather my things, smile at Donny, thank him for his help, shake his one hand, and catch up to Larry, who is already across the showroom, holding the door open for me.

It Ain't Over Till The Fat Lady Sings

We saunter over to our car. I state the obvious, "What the hell is wrong with you? Asking him if he types with his stump. Walking away over less than a thousand dollars. I got up at 5:00 a.m. I didn't shower. I'm hungry, tired, and…"

He hisses at me through clenched teeth, "Be quiet. Here he comes."

I turn around, and there's Donny, smiling, calm walking towards us. He says, "I can go up another thousand on the trade-in. Does that work for you?"

Larry acts like he needs to think it over, he stalls, rubs his chin, and finally says, "Cheryl, what do you think?"

I'm flabbergasted. I cannot believe he won't say yes himself, as if my opinion about which truck to buy, or not, carries any weight. I have half a mind to say, "Absolutely not. Let's go home. It's not good enough," and watch Larry scramble to save the deal. Bahaha.

Instead, I glance over at Donny, looking ever so hopeful, and I say, "Absolutely, it's more than fair." Did Larry raise his brow at me?

Everyone's happy, except me. I just want a hot shower, some food, and sleep.

Hours later, after I've taken on the shape of the orange plastic chair, I've been sitting in for what seems the better part of my life. Our loan is approved. The papers are signed. Our trade-in is emptied. The new truck is detailed. We've handed over a cashier's check, trade fobs, and the truck is ours.

Rumi Scores Again

I make one last coffee for the road.

Okay, the best news ever, the seats have a massage feature. I'm not kidding. All the way home, my butt and back enjoy a relaxing massage with the seat warmers on and the sunroof open to the stars. Larry even stops at Jim Boy's Taco to feed his hungry wife.

Straordinaria!

I say welcome the unexpected, because that missing truck and salesguy were just what we needed to clear the way for a better deal, and what is more delightful than an unexpected, four-hour massage?

SHE'S NOT PEDALING

"I am convinced that the jealous, the angry, the bitter and the egotistical are the first to race to the top of mountains. A confident person enjoys the journey, the people they meet along the way and sees life not as a competition. They reach the summit last because they know God isn't at the top waiting for them. He is down below helping his followers to understand that the view is glorious where ever you stand."
–Shannon Alder

I'm sorry, but I find impediments endlessly amusing. The virtue of patience is an ongoing battle for some people (we'll not mention names), and I can't stress this enough. Until it is mastered at an intermediate level, you will be at the mercy of the universe, and believe me, when I say she has a wicked sense of humor and lots of time on her hands.

Curb Your Enthusiasm

I'm still in bed. This has become my writing station of late, or I'm currently too impaired to do anything but languish on a soft mattress, feeble, inert.

And I take no responsibility for my predicament.

The muscles to the right and left of my generous butt cheeks are throbbing, most likely inflamed, not to mention my upper thighs, which have the musculature of spaghetti. Additionally, I've been fried like bacon, but I'm no longer crispy. Try not to picture it.

I'm thinking back on the weekend, a birds-eye view if you will, seeing how each moment merges seamlessly with the next as if an intentional orchestration.

But it's not. Time just refuses to stop, so it might appear to be organized, but it is simply a jumble of events, strung together as if by a child unconcerned with the complimentary order of beads.

For your enjoyment (subjectively), I'll describe each bead in minute detail, one at a time. You might refill your coffee.

If a day were to age, I would say our adventure begins at middle-age, just past the noon hour, before the sun has reached its zenith on a Thursday afternoon.

My husband's first challenge is allowing me to drive, so he can work, but the real dilemma is loading his parents into the truck while stashing all their gear in and around a monstrous tandem bike.

It's fair to say they brought the entire refrigerator, literally. I'm talking about an enormous cooler stuffed with pasta, sauce, bread, lunch meats, apples, vegetables, cheeses, crackers, condiments, and God knows what. The grumbling from my husband as he wedges the refrigerator between multiple suitcases, a cardboard box of "their" booze, cane, toiletry bags, computers, books, and our big-framed bike is nothing less than impressive.

Big Trucks Win

All aboard, Cheryl is at the helm, just like God likes it. Nana is sitting shotgun, with Nono and Larry consigned to the back. I don't know why, but every time I read that, I smile.

Nono keeps us entertained with stories of family lore, but Larry has to make several conference calls. After slipping on his EarPods, he says, "Dad, quiet. I'm on a call."

Larry Sr. says, "Oh, sorry, son, okay."

Ten minutes later, Larry says, "Dad, I'm still on a call."

Nana says, "Larry, be quiet. He's on a call."

Me, "Shush."

Larry Sr. says, "Oh, yeah, sorry."

Ten minutes later, we cover the same ground as if Ground Hog Day.

It helps to pass the time.

The highlight of the drive is when Nana and I play cat and mouse with a mini coop right before we hit the grapevine. This obnoxious mini has been weaving in and out of traffic for miles, ruthlessly cutting people off, causing all sorts of angst. What the hell? This little rat, as I've come to refer to it, shoots out of nowhere, coming up fast on my right, and she thinks I'm going to slow down and let her slide right in. Honey, we've been driving for four hours, no stops. You're messing with the wrong pussycat. I hug the bumper in front of me as if we're married. The cars behind me follow suit, and that little mini gets stuck behind a big rig. Woot Hoot. See yah!

I like big trucks, and I will not lie.

When the traffic is light, I try to make up for lost time, but we land on Marta and Ken's doorstep in the dark.

The unload is simply the reverse of the load. I decide to wait it out in the kitchen with a nice glass of wine. Total win.

Dinner is fabulous, fresh pasta, homemade sauce (now I'm grateful for the refrigerator), along with sipping wine on the patio late into the evening. Mild temperatures, not a bug in sight. No wonder this place is so popular.

Desert Destinations

After a pleasant hike in the morning, Larry and I load our suitcases back into the truck and head to Palm Springs for our first tandem event of the year.

Oh, joy.

The El Saguaro Hotel is an interesting destination, extremely retro in design, colorful, shall we say, slightly aged, and ever so crowded with wrinkle-free people sipping fruity drinks, wearing enormous hats and skimpy bathing suits.

Larry says, "Stay with the car. I'll check in, and then we'll park by our room so we can bring the bike up."

Five minutes later, he runs out to the car, clearly distressed. His hair has sprung into action, if you know what I mean. He says, "The line is a mile long, only one guy working the front desk. It's a total disaster."

"No problem. I'll wait in the air-conditioned lobby. You stay with the bike."

He squints at me as if I'm talking in a foreign language and sort of runs back to the lobby.

The sun is intense, and after sitting in the car for a brief spell, I lock it up and head inside, where it's not only cool but ever so colorful. He's right. The line is long and not moving. Everyone has a dog with them, and the solo guy at the counter is highly inefficient, not to mention clearly agitated.

The entire room cheers when a second clerk appears from the back room, and eventually, we score a key to our suite. We requested a ground-floor unit so we can store our bike in the room while we're downtown. It's sort of like having a dog, but we don't have to feed it.

Best laid plans.

Moving the car around back, we unload everything. I have the suitcases, briefcases, and books. Larry has the big dog.

The room key doesn't work.

With the patience of a two-year-old, Larry runs back to the front desk. I'm now in charge of the big dog, suitcases, books, and computers. He pushes his way to the front of the line (can you picture it?) and demands they re-key his key immediately.

That poor desk clerk didn't have a chance.

Larry returns, a little sweaty but triumphant.

Sadly, the re-keyed key doesn't work either.

Do you see where this is going?

Back to the front desk, he goes less chirpy than the last time.

Back to the room.

Still doesn't work.

Bahaha, now I need to tinkle because I've been giggling so much. Silently, of course.

A janitor takes pity on me and lets me into the room. Larry arrives, all flustered. "How the hell did you get in?"

"The janitor."

"My key still doesn't work. I'm not going to worry about it. Let's lock up and go down to the bar for a cold margarita and some chips. Then we'll drive into town and check in to our event."

You have to agree, the man knows how to turn lemons into margaritas!

I drop everything, literally, right where I stand, and say, "I'm ready."

Things are looking up.

The refreshments are refreshing as hell, and with renewed spirits, we head into town to pick up our swag and enjoy a nice dinner. We might never be able to get back into our room, but that's not the bead we're currently threading.

Herding Cats

It never gets old. I'm talking about the universe and her demented sense of humor. She really is quite creative. The entire event is organized by last names, and this year everyone's name starts with either M, N, or O.

Form one line, please.

There are heaps of volunteers sitting at empty tables with literally no lines. I move to the end of the M, N, and O's and quietly watch my husband spring into action. This is what I love about Larry. He does not accept the reality with which he is confronted. He generates his own.

Larry approaches the first volunteer, who is staring unblinkingly into the abyss, mildly unnerved by Larry's unexpected presence. This dude must have been a first-class Scout.

Larry says, "Can you help us out here, mate? Maybe borrow the M, N, O list for a second and let us check in?"

Boy Scout says, "Oh, that's not possible. We're alphabetized (nothing like stating the obvious), and I'm only trained to do H, I, J, K." Does it make you wonder what this person does for a living?

Larry smiles. It's a tad stiff and moves to the next bored volunteer. "Can you help me out…"

"No."

If anything, the universe is consistent.

Larry's confidence is disconcerting and highly entertaining, but I have to say he has a confounding success rate. As he moves down the line, I slowly move up. When he arrives at table D, E, and F, it's my turn at M, N, and O, but Larry has found a malleable person, and he waves me down.

What can you do? I abandon my place in line.

Okay, you'd think this would be a one-stop shop, but sadly, they don't distribute the jerseys we ordered for the ride tomorrow at the check-in stations. The malleable person points to another long-ass line up the street.

"That's the shirt line," she says.

Had we known, we would have divided and conquered, but it's so much better this way!

Don't you think?

Sweet Landings

For safety purposes, they blocked the street off to thru traffic. There are over 6,000 bikers signed up for this event, and they are all milling around a beer and wine garden set up by the event organizers. There's a plethora of restaurants, ranging from Mexican to Korean, Italian to Japanese, American barbeque joints, delis, and high-end steakhouses. They are all full, adorned with throngs of beautiful young people wearing spandex pants, tight butts, and absolutely zero body fat. You'd think this was Hollywood?

Where are all the middle-aged, slightly softened, gently layered people?

We mosey up to an open bar. It's outside under the stars, and we order a glass of wine.

Dinner is nothing less than extraordinary. I have the ravioli with vodka sauce, and Larry orders a penne pasta with some sort of exotic meat and cheese sauce. Why didn't I feel some sort of premonition? A delightful evening is always highly suspicious, followed by mild weather and this eerie sense of anticipation hanging in the air. But I was under the spell of the dessert and had no clue what tomorrow would bring. Thank God or I wouldn't have slept a wink. We drive back to the hotel, which has sorted out the key issue, and we are granted lawful entry to our room.

She's Not Pedaling

If you sign up for the fifty-mile ride, you need to be downtown by 8:00 a.m. sharp, queued up, and ready for action. It surprised us to see several tandem bikes in the mix, couples our age who obviously went to bed at a decent hour last night and weren't downtown partying it up with the millennials.

What a relief to know all those ambulances aren't lined up for me.

There is this intentional buildup of anticipation, excitement, and, if I were honest, fear. The local high school band is belting out a rendition of "Eye of the Tiger." People line the sidewalks with foldout chairs, waving flags, cheering us on. Between the announcements, cheerleaders, and police presence, the atmosphere is charged with feverish energy.

They let us go in packs of fifty, so we don't end up in a tangled wad, and, waiting to be released, we creep slowly up the street.

The gun fires, and an explosion of riders roll out as if a carpet of bright colors.

Larry starts us off at a mild pace. Many of the bikers pass us up, but we're not in a hurry, and I believe Larry is trying to ease my anxiety.

Let me get this out of the way right now. I'm already tired. We haven't even gone a mile, and I'm having entire conversations with myself. It's not helping.

I'm not convinced I can do this. It feels as if we're riding at a high altitude, and I can't get enough air.

Every twentieth biker feels the need to say, "She's not pedaling," as they pass us by. They think this is hysterical, and you can hear them giggling from a block away. I'm not kidding. If it's not about my pedaling (By the way, the pedals are connected. I really don't have the option not to pedal.), it's "She's reading a book. She's filing her nails. She's sleeping."

Really?

The first ten times, it was cute. Now, it's annoying, and I'm searching for snarky comebacks, but there are none. It's as if a tandem bike comes with the added bonus of nonstop commentators who feel empowered to engage with us.

Does Larry look like the friendly type?

The first fifteen miles of the tour are all uphill. I've sweated half my body weight and, just like life, when I get overwhelmed, I break it into small pieces. I've taken to staring at the ground where our momentum is most visible, deep breaths, and this seems to calm me. If I look ahead at the crest of the hill in the distance, I panic. It feels as if we're not moving at all.

Larry senses my discomfort and says, "Don't pedal so hard. Pace yourself."

"I'm okay. I just need to stay focused."

"We have a long way to go. I'm doing good. I can carry us."

Life is a tandem event if you think about it. My efforts are intimately connected to not only his ability to keep going, but our on-going momentum. We're interdependent, sometimes I carry my weight, other times he carries the both of us. Today is one of those days.

We're out of the water by mile twenty, and there are no water stations in sight. The temperature is unusually hot for this time of year. It's in the 80s, and everyone is looking for water. Larry stops at a mobile repair van parked on the side of the road and asks for water. The generous guy digs into the back of his truck, finds a half-empty gallon of water, and hands it to us. We fill our bottles (Hello? Pandemic? Ring a bell?), thank him and climb back on the big dog. I'm feel as if I might be mildly insane!

I'll admit, on the first sharp turn, I almost take us out. My instinct is to lean in the opposite direction. In my defense, it feels as if we're falling. I think I'm saving the day as I lean away with all my girth. Larry desperately fights the forces of gravity. We miss the curb by centimeters, and I receive a curt lecture on the mechanics of motion.

"You have to lean into the turn, or we're going to tank it."

"I can try?"

"You can try?"

"What do I get?"

I get the look, backward but still effective.

Some stranger says, "She's not pedaling."

Me, "Good one. Never heard that before."

By the grace of God, we make it to the first rest stop at mile twenty-five. If you've ever ridden a horse, then you'll know what I mean when I say it feels as if I've been in the saddle all day. I'm pretty sure I'll be walking funny for the rest of my natural life.

I just want some shade, but we're in the middle of the desert in a parking lot. The heat is radiating off the pavement as if we're standing on a barbeque. A large human-size grill, and I'm already fully baked, if you know what I mean.

There are tables set up with water, Gatorade, sliced oranges, bananas, and apples. Little cups of pretzels with peanut butter, nuts, and such.

Of course, there's one long-ass line, and Larry moves docilely to the end as if he was a participant in the Squid Games.

I sit with the fire ants on the curb, minding the dog. When Larry gets to the front of the line, he waves me over, and we fill up on water and snacks for the better part of three minutes before he's hankering to go. You know what I'm ready for?

Let me just say getting back on the bike is heroic. Epic. Phenomenal.

In my humble opinion.

As we exit the human barbeque, we realize we are on the top of the world, as if Rocky hitting that last step at the Philadelphia Museum of Art. It's downhill for the next ten miles, and guess who is passing everyone up? The bike that weighs the most. Yeah, baby.

We cover more miles in a couple of minutes than you can possibly imagine. I'm leaning into turns like nobody's business, gliding, pedaling, soaring across the landscape with the best of them.

"She's not pedaling."

"Because we know how to glide!"

Well, I'm sorry to say the euphoria is short-lived, and just when I think I'm Kate Courtney. There are more hills to conquer. It's eighty-eight degrees outside. I've consumed at least six bottles of water and still don't have to pee. Should I be worried?

The surrounding mountains are striking. Everywhere you look, you are confronted by majestic peaks that jet up from the ground, leaving you with the distinct feeling that something extraordinary was involved in their creation.

Around mile forty, just when I'm about to throw in the towel, scream "Uncle!" and capitulate to my warring body, we find an oasis. The second and final rest stop comes into view. There are tables and tables stacked with heaping bowls of pasta, meatloaf, mashed potatoes, tamales, fruit, liquids, nuts, pretzels, cases of water, and fresh salads. People are milling about everywhere. Rows of bike racks line the dirt field. Volunteers stand ready to guard the bikes while we eat.

Larry and I gorge on delicious tidbits for at least eight minutes before Larry wants to hit the road. I'm not sure I'm capable of riding another mile.

I'm shoving tamales in my mouth as fast as I can, fiercely shaking my head, more frantic shoving. Yes, it's a stalling tactic, but I'm desperate.

When we return begrudgingly to the bike, there's a group of guys looking at our rig. They are admiring the massive frame. You don't see this model very often as it is no longer in production. Of course, someone says, "Your nails sure look nice. You've been back there filing, Jenny." (My seat is embroidered with the name of the previous owner.)

"Oh, that is soooo funny, and you got the name wrong, too."

Male laughter masks their confusion.

If they only knew what I was thinking.

Back on the bike, I have to say the last 10 miles are absolute torture. My butt is so sore I'm forced to stand up on the pedals every few blocks to get any relief. My feet ache, even though I continually adjust their placement on the pedals. The tension in my back is excruciating, and my hands hurt from leaning on the handlebars for five hours.

I consider calling for an extra-large Uber, but the reception is bad.

Larry's like, "You've got this, babe. We're almost there, three more miles."

Me, "I don't want it. At my age, I have nothing to prove. Mile forty-seven is a win for me."

Larry, "Wait until they hand you that medal with an ice-cold beer, and you'll have something worthy to write about."

Me, "I have plenty to write about, and I don't need a participation award."

Some idiot passes us by, "She's not pedaling."

Me, "I know who you are. I'll find you, and you'll regret the day you were born."

Larry, "We might need to upgrade you to a martini?"

I can hear the band playing from a mile away. I've resorted to self-talk, but now I'm doing it out loud. Every force in the universe is consorting against me, and I'm so done.

I want shade and maybe a gallon of ice water.

After gliding into the crowd of euphoric riders, a volunteer hands us our medals, and she says, "Congratulations." I'm completely gassed.

This must qualify as a presidential accomplishment. Where the hell is Joe and Kamala?

Larry walks our bike over to a tree and rests it there. I find the nearest curb in the shade after grabbing two bottles of water right off some poor saps table. I flop down on the hard surface and drink as if I've been lost in the desert.

Wait. I have been lost in the desert.

Larry recovers quickly. He wants to take pictures. Then, we should go to the beer garden with two thousand other bikers, half of whom accused me of not pedaling.

I'm unable to move. I drink both bottles, still thirsty. Beer sounds awful! Yeah, that's a first.

So, of course, we end up in the beer garden. It's packed, nowhere to sit. Larry grabs some chairs out of a random truck and sets them in the shade. I might sleep here tonight.

Sipping beer, watching the bikers file in, smiling, high on endorphins, I watch thousands of sweaty people laughing, relaxing, and enjoying the body's opiate receptors, which somehow missed me.

It'll wear off. It's just a matter of time.

Back at the hotel, I slip out of my soaked bike pants into dry pajama bottoms. I'm too tired to shower or change my sweaty shirt, so I crawl into bed just as I am.

AARP On The Move

Larry wakes me up hours later. I can't remember who, what, or where I am. It's dusk.

Larry says, "Get in the shower. We have reservations at the steak house tonight, and it's almost time to go."

"Who are you?"

"I'm the one who pedaled."

"Oh, honey, don't go there."

Downtown is hopping with all those happy endorphin-laden people, most of whom stayed in their biking gear and obviously never left the beer garden.

We're slightly early, so we enjoy a cool glass of wine at a swanky Italian bar along the strip. We order juicy melon with prosciutto, burrata cheese, and crostini. I'm no longer in need of a priest for last rites, because obviously I'm in heaven. I think those endorphins finally kicked in, or the wine, maybe both.

The Final Bead

The next morning, I feel worn out, deflated, as if an old tire, but I keep rolling. We pack our bags, load the car, and head to Sherman's for breakfast. I have my priorities.

Sherman's is a famous bakery and deli. The food is outstanding, and it feels good to linger over endless cups of coffee and succulent eggs benedict when my body feels as if it's a refugee in a foreign country.

We arrive at Marta and Ken's in time to watch the Superbowl, munch on chicken wings, barbequed hamburgers, and cheer on our favorite teams. I have no preference.

I'm just glad to be alive.

Glancing over at Larry, to the guy with whom I'm doing this life in tandem, and I'm grateful to have such a capable man on my team. The mystery of life isn't about coordinating the pedaling. It's finding someone worth pedaling for and one who is willing to carry the entire load when need be. That's the final bead.

Oh, and I wore my medal all night!

WHAT DO I REALLY WANT?

"Ripples on the surface of the water were silver salmon passing under—different from the ripples caused by breezes."
–Gary Snyder

I'm floating on the lake, suspended, cool, lethargic. It's been a lovely week, but the truth is I'm exhausted. Those soft words of Gary Snyder keep rippling across my mind, pushing my thoughts to the edge. I laugh at myself. The trappings of illusionary boundaries, they don't exist, and I might need some sleep.

It's deep where I am, forcing me to consider the divergent causes of the water's movement, often undetectable but efficacious, as if desire, want, and need were all converging in the same location. I love the fact I can float away from it all, distance myself from the rigors of life, but the truth is catfish jump. Rafts deflate. Waterlogged is a real thing.

All weekend I have been observing how people maneuver in the world. To me, this is fascinating. How does he manipulate the situation to get what he wants? What is he willing to risk? How does she manage to look completely at ease when surrounded by chaos? Why do her actions conflict so powerfully with her words? How do we justify our anger? What biases or assumptions is he working from to have formed such an adamant opinion? Those who've mastered distraction, what are they hiding, avoiding? She weaves an interesting story, but to what avail? Criticism is so revealing, is it not? Laughter is rich, draws me in, like being caught in a web, only it's not Charlotte's.

What do people really want? It's confusing and complicated to figure humans out because we change with the circumstances as if chameleons. We camouflage our real purpose and hope we won't be detected. Maybe we're afraid of rejection, ridicule, or, worse, humiliation? *We shift our allegiance, as if immigrants in our own bodies, and wonder where we belong.*

I think a lot about who I am and the stories I tell. I'm a writer. I aim for authenticity, but when I fall short, it's as clear as the pimple on my face. I know, pop that thing, slap on some cover-up.

As I drift further and further away from my home, beach, and boundaries, so do my thoughts. Why am I in such conflict with what I really want? Being a human is far from simplistic. Like statistics, it's confusing, and our data is hopelessly flawed.

Authenticity is everything! Because when you wake up in the morning and look in the mirror, you want to be proud of the person you're reflecting, or at least not mortified. And that is only possible if you're being honest with yourself, compassionate, and ever so forgiving. It's the basis of friendship, and that took a while for me to learn.

I want a house full of family, but time to write and think. I want endless cups of coffee without indigestion. I want a spotless environment but for everyone to be comfortable. I want lots of wide brimed hats, but I don't want to store them.

I want sunshine on a crisp morning. I want clean windows, except for the handprints of my grandchildren. I want rows of deck chairs filled with good people, kind, gentle, sincere, but oh, how boring that would be.

I want the conflict of sand on the beach and glistening kitchen floors, but that would mean no one who ventures out could come back in, the exact opposite of what I want.

I want to weed out my closet, remodel the kitchen, and a pounded copper table for twelve, without the expense or stress of procuring such things.

I want the laundry done, folded, stacked, and ready for use without having to do it. I want the pantry stocked with alphabetized can goods, stacks of clean white paper plates, and extra peanut butter but then I'd be living someone else's life.

I want everyone doing exactly what they want, but without my assistance. That could be a lie.

I want fireworks, soft beach towels, starry nights, and waves lapping against the shore but not the fires, wind, and heat of July.

I want more holidays, time, and bird feeders, which makes me want my mom.

I want her order, her smell, her safety, her Ruth Ann Severance kind of sovereign love. I want the heaviness out of my heart, but not the experience of love. Shit.

I caught my reflection in the mirror this morning. I said to myself, "It's okay, not great." This made me laugh. And there she was, my mom, a glimpse. Has she been there all the time?

I'll take her ghost, the lady of the lake, the ashes of the dead. A jar harboring an entire life, but not really. She lingers in the air, but I cannot breathe her in. Thank God for Nancy. She has her eyes, eyes that love me.

Oh, how I long for healthy wit, wisdom, and long, lean legs. Never to be compliant, but ready to welcome.

I want traffic, not in my life but in the blog. I want words that curl up on my lap and force me to appreciate them. But I don't want my thoughts domesticated.

I want Shaggy, confidence, and long summer nights but I abhor transience. I want shade, twinkle lights, and breakfast in bed. Who doesn't? I want my apple phone close but without all the distractions.

I want dark chocolate, jeans that fit just right, and that man I met as a boy kissing me goodnight. As if wine, I want you to want me like I want you.

I want Bonfires, s'mores, bats but without the rice flies. And I want Tony. I want him to come home, even though I hate the thought of destroying his dreams. Someday he'll wake up and realize family is the dream.

I want romcoms, like *When Harry Met Sally*, and lots of popcorn. Fingers slick with melted butter, ice-cold Pepsi, and a cloth napkin. I want to weigh the same at the beginning of the week as I do at the end. Bahaha...

I want no clutter. That's not true. I want cute clutter that remains dusted, charming, and of service. Like blue mason jars, vintage ice buckets, scented candles, and succulents lounging in chipped teacups. Mind your own fantasies.

I want more birthdays, soft breezes, the reflection of the moon on the water, fast internet, and crisp bacon. Did I mention my dad? He took a piece of my heart when he left. Never far from my thoughts or dreams. Oh, how I miss his mischievous smile.

I want the words to land on the page in perfect order, as if a gentle rain, without sweat, strain, or editing.

I've given a thousand kisses this week. I want more of Audrey, Sienna, and Cora, but oh, how I enjoyed sleeping in this morning, which reminds me of soft beds, soft sheets, and my eyes opening after sunrise.

I want to sit on the deck, wine in hand, laughter, listening to the chimes of my people. Feeling the wind in my hair, eyes following the flight of winged ones, heart-melting with joy.

Is that too much to ask?

I didn't think so.

EPILOGUE

"Hope... A few Stories yet to be completed! Perhaps. A side yet to be unfolded, filled, completed... Finished!"
–Tahreem Rahat

This morning, as I write these words, it's currently 4:44 a.m. I couldn't sleep. Larry and I slipped between the sheets with an unresolved issue between us. It was one of those restless nights, so I got up, opened my MacBook, and gave my fingers free rein.

We're up at the lake for the weekend. I'm snuggled in the doublewide, wrapped in my fur blanket, staring out the window into the inky darkness. It's as comforting as a womb.

I love the quiet of the early morning, the brisk air, the clarity of thought not yet clouded by the demands of the day, disappointments, and all those irreconcilable differences that stay moored in our stubborn hearts. This much I know to be true. When I overindulge in righteousness, I wake up with a moral hangover.

Caffeine might help.

As I make my way from the warm bed to the kitchen in search of coffee. It reminds me of navigating life without a map. I know where most of the obstacles are situated in this house, but often it's the ones that move between people that cause us to stumble.

I had hoped by now we had reached an age where we existed beyond our differences, as Rumi notes, "Out beyond ideas of wrongdoing and rightdoing, there is a field. I'll meet you there." I can't help but wonder if such a place exists.

As the moon beam forms a river of denial across the waters of truth, I defer to her illumination. I know, morning philosophers are the worst. There's just enough light to secure a mug without turning on the harsh fluorescents. I switch on the coffee pot and wait as the hot water slowly presses through the course grounds. The aroma is divine.

While the coffee brews, I know something is missing, and my hand naturally feels around for Shaggy, who would have been glued to my side on a morning such as this. He would have been looking up at me with those floppy ears pricked forward, wondering what the hell I'm doing up in the middle of the night. I miss the way he flopped at my feet and nuzzled my hand when he needed to be scratched behind the ears, but mostly, how his pure love was given without expectations. Some refer to that as agape love. We strive for this as humans, but often fail.

The sun will be rising soon. She will slip off her veil of darkness and greet the new day naked, reborn, absolved. I envy her.

I plan on embracing all that after I finish today's Wordle.

With coffee in hand, I return to my chair of inequity and wrangle with my wayward thoughts. My mind wanders to an appointment I have with the DMV to renew my license, the one that will be required if I ever hope to travel. The DMV in Lakeport is a hell of a lot less crowded than in San Jose, so I made an appointment last week and gathered my documents. I realize this might be the last picture I ever take for a driver's license, and I'm not sure how I feel about that. Maybe I should wash my hair?

After the DMV, I have a Zoom call with Kara, my editor. We're going to pour over a rough draft of the book you're now holding in your hand. I've been playing hide and seek with this dream for years. It's time. I've opened my eyes, and now I see she's the hope that has been hiding beneath my fears and reservations. As Annie Dillard claims, "I think it would be well, and proper, and obedient, and pure, to grasp your one necessity and not let it go, to dangle from it limp wherever it takes you."

It is my deepest desire that the contents of this manuscript fulfill some sort of need in the world, even if it's just one person, one story, or one word that helps us understand we're not alone. We're all laboring to bring forth the person we were meant to be with our legs crossed.

As I allow my eyes to caress the sable room, I'm remembering where I was over a decade ago when we bought this place. It was the summer after my dad died. Larry, Dante, and I scooped up my mom in the Northwest and took her on an impromptu adventure, a road trip along the rustic coastal highways of the Northwest. We added Forks to the itinerary because Dante had a thing for Bella. It was the first night of our journey. We were having dinner at dad's favorite restaurant, *Calvin's Crab House,* on the shores of Sequim.

The first sip of wine is always the best. We sent up a toast to dad, ordered our favorite seafood, and while we're musing over tomorrow's itinerary, Larry's phone rings. He excuses himself from the table to take the call outside. I remember when he returned, his face was ashen, as if he'd seen a ghost.

With enormous dread, I say, "What happened?"

Did I detect a hint of a smile? He says, "I think we just bought a lake house."

Larry's parents built a house on Clearlake when we were still in high school. It has been a favorite place for the Oreglia clan to gather for years. As our tribe expanded and the family compound could no longer accommodate us all, we went in search of a home of our own. From 1995 to 2010, we searched for an affordable home on the lake. We made six offers during *the hunting years,* as I refer to them, all rejected. God bless Scott, our realtor, he never gave up. One of the last offers we made was for the house we would eventually own.

Bud Brown was looking to sell his home in the same subdivision as Larry's parents, but as if an ostrich, he obstinately ignored the economic crisis. The price he set for his home was double that of the current market rate. I was angry at Scott for showing us a house we couldn't afford, but we threw caution to the wind and put in a fair offer. It was outright refused. In fact, Bud did not budge on a single dollar, so we made a polite exit and went our separate ways.

That was two years ago. Expect delays. God is planning.

I say, "What house?"

"The Tulip House (named after the winery Bud owned) in Kono Tayee."

"Wasn't that out of our reach?"

"It was Scott who called. He said Bud has since passed away. His five kids want to sell. We were the only offer they received in two years, and they want to know if we're still interested."

"And you said yes?"

"I did."

"Holy shit." With every fiber of my being, I felt like my dad had a hand in this unexpected turn of events, as if him and Bud were throwing one back in some heavenly tavern.

Unprovoked, mom says, "Your dad sure knows how to close a deal," and returns to her pan-fried filet of sole.

Larry didn't eat a bite of his dinner that night. When we got back to the lodge, we used the fax machine in the hotel bar to sign the offer, which was accepted by the Brown family. Then, we ordered double martinis and tried to remember what the house looked like, worried about the affordability of such a luxury.

When we finally gained access to the home we purchased from a bar in Washington, both of us just walked silently from room to room, discovering it anew. I believe we kissed as we encountered each other in the main hall. We knew what we had and what this would mean for our family, but we were also acutely aware that the death of Bud Brown was what made this possible, and that was difficult to process.

Later that night, I was snooping through an old dresser in the master suite. I found a picture of the entire Brown family in the back of the drawer. I have it perched against a stack of books in our room. Every time I pass, I move my hand from lip to picture, thanking them for the privilege of this space.

Before my family arrived for our first weekend at the lake, Nancy, mom, my girlfriend Christine, and I took a few days to clean out the new digs from the previous owners. When I turned the key in the lock and pushed open the front door, Nancy and mom both got a little misty. They said, "dad would have loved this place."

We came armed with new bedding, all muted and matching, with detergent to wash the towels, dishes, and utensils. We spent half the day rearranging the furniture, replacing artwork, and fussing over the placement of trinkets. In a day, we made it our own. A quick trip to Safeway in Lakeport had the pantry refilled and bathrooms restocked with toilet paper, soap, and shampoo. Nancy vacuumed. I mopped. Chris dusted, with mom directing the entire production from her place on the couch.

By afternoon, we were spent, so we gathered on mismatched deck chairs and opened some wine.

Chris says, "We're going to have to burn some sage to chase away any bad energy that might be lingering."

Nancy says, "Where in the world are we going to get that?"

Chris says, "I brought some."

I say, "Of course you did."

Mom says, "Hand me a torch. I'll clear out the back rooms."

Nancy says, "You think there are actual spirits hanging around the house?"

Chris says, "Not after we're finished."

I say, "I think death is going to be the greatest adventure of all…"

They all look at me as if I'm insane, which might be true.

My mom passed away in the middle of the night on June 14, 2017. Nancy and I were huddled together in her generous bed, not ten feet from the hospital bed we set up in the living room. George Winston was playing softly in the background, the same music that accompanied my dad from this life to the next. I'd been sleeping there in the same clothes for four days, having raced home from the lake after a call from my sister alerting me of mom's deteriorating condition. My last words to mom were, "I love you." She was no longer fully alert, but she took my hand, and I knew she knew.

The night after she died, I had a dream. I was racing around the house trying to find my shoes and car keys, all in a panic, running late. I was supposed to meet my parents at the train station.

After I park the car, I start running, but I'm not covering any ground.

I can see them in the distance. They're younger than I remember, holding hands, waiting patiently on the platform for me to join them. My dad is dressed in pressed khaki slacks, a Pendleton shirt, and wide suspenders. Mom is wearing a sundress adorned with colorful hummingbirds, as if wrapped in a roll of wallpaper. They wave enthusiastically when they see me.

When I wake up, I realize they'll be there when I die, just as they were at my birth. I don't know why I know this, but I do. I'll need them in the next life as much as I did in the present. This is how love repeatedly circles back on itself, "As it was in the beginning, is now, and ever shall be, world without end."

But in the meantime, we're living in the gap between the two extremes. As Lauren Klarfeld says, "… people are only guests in your story—the same way you are only a guest in theirs—so make the chapters worth reading." I love that.

I love living life from two places, our home in the suburbs and our home on the lake. Two completely different worlds, much like the contrast between my life as a young mother and the one I live in now. My home in the Bay Area entombs the memories of a new marriage, raising the kids, working, sometimes failing, often thriving before gently kicking everyone out of the nest. The lake is my present (take that any way you want). It gathers my chicks from all corners of the world, brings us together, and accompanies us in this new season of life. One where I'm encouraged to embrace the grey hair, gently layered middle, and wrinkled epidermis that still manages to hold me together.

A new awareness rises up in me as the sun is peeking over the rim of the eastern hills. I recognize the senselessness of allowing an argument to slip between us, to diminish one minute of our precious time, to leave either of us feeling lost and forlorn. I hear those familiar footsteps coming down the hall. Larry approaches me with hesitancy but bravely leans in for a kiss, and that is how we meet in the field beyond ideas of wrongdoing and rightdoing, for now...

It has been an honor to have you accompany me during this season of life. Hopefully, we'll indulge in many bouts of brazen laughter, sip good wine, eat well, argue some, and burn a little sage until we enter our final labor from this life to the next.

From the clamor of the city to the gentle shores of the lake, we were never designed to live in isolation. People need not only validation, but camaraderie, compassion, and a loyal dog. This life is not what I imagined. It's so much more, so I'm trying to let the future unfold organically instead of tarnishing it with my limitations. At times, I feel small, separate, and alone, but the truth is we've never been more connected. *Grow Damn It* is a philosophy. It's about survival, breaking through the barriers that confine us, thriving as if weeds, rooted in the soil of life.

I look up from what I am writing. The room is aglow with soft morning light, and I'm swaddled in a moment of sheer gratitude, gazing at a field of golden poppies growing wild on the rocky beach.

The End

ACKNOWLEDGMENTS

If this is going to be a proper dedication, I'm compelled to prioritize my parents, Ann and Dick Johnson, who dragged me to the library every week, bought me a writing desk before I could write, and kept every letter I ever wrote to them bundled in ribbons. Although they've moved to a more ethereal place, they are never far from my thoughts, my heart, and my dreams.

Writing is a unique occupation. You're basically a secretary attempting to capture the cascade of thoughts flowing from one's precarious mind. One day, my sister, Nancy Wood, asked me to share these captive thoughts with the world. She's older and wiser, so I did what I was told. And I can't thank her enough. Love you, my darling sister.

Now I don't want to over-inflate the importance of a spouse, but from day one, Larry has been an endless source of material. His unconventional, flamboyant, high-octane lifestyle is the backbone of my work. Perfect marriages make for boring copy, and ours is as flawed and fabulous as the next. Thank you for riding in tandem with me, letting me be the stoker while you carry the heavy load, and hanging in there when the road gets rocky. After all these years, I'm still madly in love.

I'd be remiss if I didn't thank my greatest treasures in life, my children and their spouses, Julie, Nic, Kelley, Tim, Tony, Thalita (not official), and Dante, for all their encouragement, critiques (even when unsolicited), suggestions, technical support, and concern over the movie rights of this work. You are my heart.

Then there are the littles, Audrey, Cora, and Sienna, grandchildren, the pinnacle of a well-lived life, and an endless source of snuggles, giggles, and kisses. You make this life unbearably sweet, you make the chambers of my heart flutter, and my gratitude swells. Love you to the moon and back.

Of course, these stories were inspired by a host of beloved family and friends who continue to inspire and encourage this crazy dream of mine, and although it is impossible to name you all, there are a few standouts who have championed me from the day I hit publish, and my first blog went live. You know who you are, my gratitude runs deep, and my love for you overflows.

A special shout out to Kara Masters, who took this untamed manuscript and domesticated the uncultivated passages. She tackled my comma abuse, run-on sentences, and conflicting tenses with grace and style. Her intuitive nature and kind disposition made collaboration a joy. I owe her so very much.

I can't thank Black Rose Writers enough for taking a chance on this unknown author, pulling my query from the herd of submissions, and giving me just enough free range to explore my options but not get lost. I'm especially grateful for the creativity and support of David King, the Black Rose staff, especially Reagan Rothe. Your courage and generosity have been a dream come true.

It gives me enormous pleasure to offer thanks and praise to the Word Press writing community for their generous support through the years. I'm ever so grateful that you take the time to read my blog and wrestle with me in the comments each week. It is a privilege to be part of your village. As always, wrapping you in love and hugs.

And finally, thank you to the Mighty Geckos, who have been encouraging me every Wednesday evening for years; to dive deeper, think bigger, and grow, damn it. They held this book in their hands when it was a shapeless vision and demanded I make it a reality. Thank you, Daniel, Jeandre, Josh, Leanne, Luke, Mary Ellen, Tasha, and Yijun. I love you.

NOTES ON LAKE COUNTY WINERIES

Six Sigma Ranch, Vineyard, and Estate Winery is one of our most beloved, located southeast of Lower Lake at 13372 Spruce Grove Road, Lower Lake. A gregarious man name Kaj and his wife Else, established Six Sigma Winery, whose motto is to make the customer feel welcome, celebrated, and valued. It's not just the usual wine tasting experience, it's an unforgettable event, one where the owner takes the time to stop by your table and chat it up with his guests. At Six Sigma, "Our team works hard toward one common goal: Making wine of extraordinary quality at an affordable price. Our story is in every single bottle of Six Sigma wine," says Kaj Ahlmann. I'd say they're a novel success and one we are driven to return to time and time again.

Vigilance Vineyards and Winery, just twenty miles down the road, is located at 13888 Point Lakeview Road, Lower Lake, and is owned by the famous winemaker Shannon Clay. They have a diverse variety of fabulous wines available to taste, enjoy with a picnic, or pair with dinner. The tasting room is a rustic old farmhouse that was once home to one of Lake County's pioneering families, and as a bonus, there are spectacular panoramic views overlooking Anderson Marsh State Park. It doesn't get better than this.

Gregory Graham Winery, less than half a mile up the street from Vigilance, at 13633 Point Lakeview Road, Lower Lake. Owned by none other than Gregory and his wife, Marianne. The tasting room is simple, but the wines are complex, something to be savored with a good meal and close friends. The first time we visited this winery, Larry and I were celebrating our anniversary, and we asked Gregory to snap a picture of us. I assumed he was one of the friendly staff. He smiled graciously, took a few shots of us, and then introduced himself as the owner. Slightly mortified, we enjoyed a tasting and a chat with Gregory and Marianne. The welcoming and friendly atmosphere had us signing up for more. We've been proud members for over ten years.

Laujor Estate Winery, located at 8664 Seigler Springs North Road, Kelseyville. The winemaker Cheryl Lucido and her husband David own this beautiful winery, one of the few wineries on the lake to boast of a wine cave. I have to say, aside from a variety of fabulous wines (we have several favorites), Cheryl and Dave are the main attractions. I remember dropping by during the middle of the week. Cheryl and Dave were juggling several tasks but stopped what they were doing to sit down and enjoy a glass of wine with us. These are salt-of-the-earth people, inviting, and gregarious. The views from the tasting room are extraordinary and a must-see if you are ever in Lake County.

Boatique Winery, just up the road from Laujor, is not one to miss. They are located at 8255 Red Hills Road, Kelseyville. The wines are wonderful and complex. They have an adorable tasting room and friendly staff who go out of their way to make you feel welcome. The tasting room is connected to a large warehouse and on display is the largest collection of refurbished wooden boats on the west coast! When you visit, you just grab a glass of bubbly and wander around the warehouse, admiring both the boats and the exceptional views from their back patio.

The beautiful **Brassfield Estate Winery**, located in California's High Valley Appellation at 10915 High Valley Road, Clearlake Oaks. Brassfield is a treat to the palate and the eyes. It has one of the largest wine caves in the world; the tasting room is a three-story Mediterranean structure with landscaped picnic areas and charming gardens. The staff is delightful. They greet you by name, always have a new varietal for you to try, and some friendly banter for your enjoyment. They repurposed the chandelier over the generous bar from the Bank of America Building in San Francisco and a fountain from the estate of no other than Clark Gable. The wines are spectacular, but we come for the people of Brassfield.

Cache Creek Vineyards and Winery, located in a restored water tower off the twenty at 250 New Long Valley Road, Clearlake Oaks. The emblem on their bottles is the elegant moose. We enjoy bringing the entire family to this establishment, as children and dogs are always welcome. The staff caters to your every need, including a bowl of water for the dog and lawn games for the family. We are a huge fan of their specialty wines, especially the bubbly and cabernet varietals. They host many enjoyable events, but their concert series outside under the stars is the highlight of the summer.

ABOUT THE AUTHOR

Cheryl Oreglia is in the prime of her life, she claims this is not up for debate, a recently retired educator, married for forty years to the guy she met in high school. Together they have raised four exigent children, who blessed them with a trio of granddaughters, along with a couple of dogs, and one sassy cat. Oreglia entered a masters program as she was entering menopause sweating her way through a MA and into a second career. She has been hosting a blog entitled *Living in the Gap*, at cheryloreglia.blog, that was acknowledged by Krista Tippett and five thousand followers on Twitter.

Grow Damn It! is a compilation of her most beloved essays tackling not only the frivolous, but the more challenging aspects of life. Oreglia lives in California with her husband.

NOTE FROM THE AUTHOR

Word-of-mouth is crucial for any author to succeed. If you enjoyed *Grow Damn It!*, please leave a review online—anywhere you are able. Even if it's just a sentence or two. It would make all the difference and would be very much appreciated.
 Thanks!
 Cheryl Oreglia

We hope you enjoyed reading this title from:

www.blackrosewriting.com

Subscribe to our mailing list – *The Rosevine* – and receive **FREE** books, daily deals, and stay current with news about upcoming releases and our hottest authors.
Scan the QR code below to sign up.

Already a subscriber? Please accept a sincere thank you for being a fan of Black Rose Writing authors.

View other Black Rose Writing titles at www.blackrosewriting.com/books and use promo code **PRINT** to receive a **20% discount** when purchasing.

www.ingramcontent.com/pod-product-compliance
Lightning Source LLC
Chambersburg PA
CBHW072001070526
44583CB00015B/1279